T0287769

E. Franklin Frazier and *Black Bourgeoisie*

E. Franklin Frazier

and

Black Bourgeoisie

Edited with an Introduction
by James E. Teele

University of Missouri Press
Columbia

University of Missouri Press, Columbia, Missouri 65211
Printed and bound in the United States of America

First paperback printing, 2018

Library of Congress Cataloging-in-Publication Data

E. Franklin Frazier and Black bourgeoisie / edited with an introduction by James E. Teele.
p. cm.
Includes bibliographical references and index.
ISBN 978-0-8262-2150-6 (paperback : alk. paper)
1. Frazier, Edward Franklin, 1894–1962. Bourgeoisie noire. 2. African Americans—Social conditions—To 1964. 3. Middle class—United States. 4. United States—Social conditions—1960–1980. 5. United States—Race relations. 6. Frazier, Edward Franklin, 1894–1962. 7. African American intellectuals—Biography. 8. African American sociologists—Biography. I. Teele, James E.
E185.86.F7283 E2 2002
305.896'073—dc21 2002017954

∞™ This paper meets the requirements of the American National Standard for Permanence of Paper for Printed Library Materials, Z39.48, 1984.

Typefaces: Palatino & Caslon

The University of Missouri Press gratefully acknowledges support from Boston University in the publication of this book.

Dedicated to

Alma, Ruth, Frances, and Francella

Contents

Acknowledgments

In a collaborative effort many people play important roles. I must begin by thanking Adelaide Cromwell, founding director of Afro-American studies at Boston University, for her inspiration, encouragement, and support in the effort to publish this work. The process started in the early 1990s when she, Wilson Moses (her successor as director), and I organized and presided over a one-day symposium that analyzed E. Franklin Frazier's *Black Bourgeoisie.* Five of the authors whose essays are included in this volume—Adelaide Cromwell, John Bracey, Martin Kilson, Wornie Reed, and Robert Hall—produced papers for that program. Later, Adelaide Cromwell suggested that I expand on our program and produce a book on Frazier's controversial work. Subsequently, the initial contributors were asked to revise their presentations for publication, and four additional scholars—Michael Winston, Hylan Lewis, Anthony Platt, and John Hope Franklin—were invited to contribute papers. Winston initially presented his paper at the meeting of the African Studies Association on November 3, 1990; Lewis was asked to prepare a paper on Frazier's early years at Howard University; Platt adapted his contribution from his book *E. Franklin Frazier Reconsidered;* Franklin graciously agreed to share some of his experiences as Frazier's student, colleague, and friend. First and foremost, I am grateful to the contributors; their creativity, dedication, and response to the editor's and reviewers' suggestions made this volume possible.

I wish to express my deep appreciation to both the Association of Black Sociologists and the American Sociological Association for inviting me to organize and preside over a special panel on Frazier at the ASA meeting in August 2000. This panel brought together Andrew Billingsley, Platt, Cheryl Gilkes, Clovis Semmes, and Stanford Lyman, and their discussion ranged widely over Frazier's signal contributions to sociology, social work, and the larger society. Panel members, with their outstanding analyses of Frazier, helped to sharpen my understanding of Frazier, and I am convinced that their views have contributed significantly to my editorial performance.

I am also indebted to Boston University, which served as the setting for our initial symposium. Dennis Berkey, the Provost of Boston University, provided special funds to me that greatly aided in all the project's indispensable tasks—manuscript preparation, travel to several conferences for the purpose of meeting with prospective contributors, and editorial assistance.

Library staff at Boston University, Virginia Union University, and Howard University and in the town of Ipswich, Massachusetts, were quite helpful in providing requested assistance at various stages in this project.

My wife, Ann Skendall Teele, was, as always, highly supportive of my work. However, in this case, I am especially grateful to her for encouraging me to take on the Frazier project. Edgar F. Borgatta, of the University of Washington, also encouraged me to undertake this task. Borgatta, a graduate student at New York University when Frazier was a visiting scholar there, spoke admiringly of Frazier's performance and popularity.

I am especially appreciative, too, of all the help I received in manuscript preparation from the sociology department staff at Boston University: Kimberly Warren, Maddie Goodwin, Katie McNamara, and Joshua Kaplan. I also received invaluable editorial assistance from Leslie Tebbe, a recent Boston University graduate and one of my former students.

Finally, I cannot say enough about the fine editorial assistance I received from the staff at the University of Missouri Press. I am especially grateful to Beverly Jarrett, the director and editor-in-chief, for her constant support and encouragement and to Jane Lago, managing editor, and Sara Davis, both for their knowledge and their readiness to help me through the editing process.

E. Franklin Frazier
and
Black Bourgeoisie

Introduction

JAMES E. TEELE

For this essay collection, a group of distinguished scholars set out to reexamine and clarify, for themselves at least, some of the work of E. Franklin Frazier, a highly acclaimed sociologist. Despite E. Franklin Frazier's status in American sociology there has been surprisingly little study of his work. While scholars have frequently referred to his work on the black family and he has been the subject of at least four doctoral dissertations, there has been only one book about his life and surprisingly little study of his work. In the biography, Anthony Platt observes that assessments of Frazier have generally denied the complexities, the uniqueness, and the consistency of the themes that preoccupied him.[1]

There is much to be gained from a close examination of Frazier. In this volume, essays by a number of distinguished scholars focus on the complexities of *Black Bourgeoisie,* Frazier's most controversial and perhaps least understood work, rather than attempting to analyze his entire body of work. This concentration is relevant to the growing concerns about problems in our cities, about the limitations and advantages of affirmative action, about racism, and about the need for community. It also reflects a renewed interest in Frazier demonstrated by the publication of new editions of his work, the naming of a Howard University research center in his honor, and the aforementioned American Sociological Association/Association of Black Sociologists joint session. Increasingly, Frazier is being studied by students in history, sociology, political science, psychology, and African American studies.

This diverse audience recognizes that all of these disciplines were used by Frazier in his work on race relations, the family, and black

1. Anthony Platt, *E. Franklin Frazier Reconsidered* (New Brunswick, N.J.: Rutgers University Press, 1991).

community life and that he invariably addressed important questions in his work, thus leading him to assume the different roles of activist and theorist, detached scholar, and radical advocate of social change at various times in his life. Therefore, this volume should be of interest to policymakers and activists as well as scholars.

At present, there is a good deal of attention focused on the responsibility of scientists, including social scientists, to see the connections between theory and practice, to understand the policy implications of their research findings, and, especially, to undertake the examination of important questions. E. Franklin Frazier's major contribution, perhaps, was that he pondered all of these issues when others did not. But he may also have imposed this responsibility and accountability on black leaders, black intellectuals, and on blacks of economic substance, and found them wanting.

Indeed, when Frazier left Atlanta to protest oppression, he embarked on a prolonged period of scholarship during which his more affective (activist) needs became secondary to his need to probe more deeply into sociological research. It could be surmised that *Black Bourgeoisie* was a reaction to this hiatus and to his annoyance that other black leaders seemed too acquiescent. Or was it?

In any analysis, witnesses offer important insights. This book includes accounts by five contributors who had scholarly, collegial, or personal relationships with Frazier. Their descriptions and recollections of discussions with him will surely enlighten our understanding of *Black Bourgeoisie.*

When E. F. Frazier was elected president of the American Sociological Association in 1948 (five years after he had served as president of the Eastern Sociological Society), he was already recognized as the leading scholar on the black family and one of the important theorists absorbed in the dynamics of social change and race relations. "Black" did not appear to be a limiting description in the appraisal of Frazier's work. Frazier was judged on his merits and was known as well for applying tough standards in evaluating the merits of his peers and students. By 1948, he had published over fifty articles and four major books, including the acclaimed *The Negro Family in the United States,* published in 1939 by the University of Chicago Press.

Frazier's early years were marked by articles reflecting his interest in social protest, social change, social work, and cooperative movements, especially as these processes applied to the black community. Later, Frazier was attracted to the idea that "knowledge would set you free," an idea strengthened during his study at the University of Chicago. In short, he came to see himself as a *scholar*, properly detached, as required by the academy. His election to the presidency of the distinguished American Sociological Association justified his dedication to sociology and certainly predicted a continuation of his single-minded devotion to the field.

However, Frazier's devotion to scholarship seemed to diminish with the appearance of *Bourgeoisie Noire*, published in France in 1955; it appeared in America two years later as *Black Bourgeoisie*. This book was seen by many as an attack on the black middle class and suggested that Frazier the scholar had disappeared. Frazier apparently had donned his protest clothes again, but this time his anger was not focused on whites who discriminated against and suppressed the black community; this time his scathing prose was focused on his own people and, most important, on black leadership. Frazier's presidency had metamorphosed into a bully pulpit, used to scold the new black middle class, including, but not limited to, the intellectuals.

Just what was *Black Bourgeoisie* about? The book described the evolution of the old black middle class from one in which genteel manners, folk traditions, and religious practices were central to one in which traditional values were less important and the outlook more secular. This new class (measured by occupational status and income level), while dependent upon the patronage of lower-class Negroes, lacked a firm place in the American economy, according to Frazier. Yet the black bourgeoisie looked down upon the black masses and scorned their culture. They even disassociated themselves from the majority of Negroes in their rejection of both their African roots and their slave past. In turn the black bourgeoisie were rejected by whites, and so they were culturally rootless and beset by feelings of inferiority and self-hatred.

So while the black masses were experiencing various problems following migration to cities (crime, delinquency, broken families), the new black middle class was experiencing a distortion of values. Its preoccupation with status, in imitation of the white upper class, led Frazier to charge it with being interested in "status without substance." Indeed, he suggested that while members of the black bourgeoisie wished to be accepted by whites, they feared competing against them, preferring segregated, safe lives, where they could excuse and hide their deficiencies. They retreated into a "world of make-believe," engaging in fantasizing and mythmaking about the extent of their successes, especially in business. They supported these illusions by indulging in "conspicuous consumption," which they could not afford. Perhaps surprisingly, Frazier says the Negro colleges and their faculty exhibited a lack of intellectual interest and joined in the pursuit of an extravagant life. Thus this class, including its intellectuals, was not only marked by a thinly veiled self-indulgence ("foolishness" to Frazier), but also failed to provide leadership for the unknowing Negro masses. The black bourgeoisie, he suggested, failed to perform the functions of a responsible elite in a minority group and have become "exaggerated" Americans.[2]

A main contributor to this false framework was the Negro press, he says. Frazier noted that while the press had started in the nineteenth century as a medium concerned with the abolition of slavery and protest of civil discrimination against blacks, it had changed after World War II into a vehicle proclaiming Negro achievements. In an explosive commentary about the role of the Negro media in this mythmaking, Frazier writes:

> The Negro press reveals the inferiority complex of the black bourgeoisie and provides a documentation of the attempts of this class to seek compensations for its hurt self-esteem and exclusion from American life. Its exaggerations concerning the economic well-being and cultural achievements of Negroes, its emphasis upon Negro "society" all tend to create a world of make-believe into which the black bourgeoisie can escape from its inferiority and inconsequence in American society.[3]

In the final chapters of the book, Frazier paints a picture of the gaudy lifestyles, conspicuous-consumption patterns, delusions, and masks that, to him, at least, indexed the make-believe world of the black bourgeoisie.

Frazier's book apparently received mainly negative reviews when it appeared, first as *Bourgeoisie Noire* and then as *Black Bourgeoisie.*

2. E. Franklin Frazier, *Black Bourgeoisie* (New York: Collier Books, 1962), 193.
3. Ibid., 146.

In a devastating review of the former, W. M. Brewer said that the book, in its selection of records, was comparable in some respects to Ulrich B. Phillips's *American Negro Slavery,* a book which assumed that Negroes were innately inferior![4] Brewer, among other criticisms, said that (1) the book restricted its findings chiefly to failures and studiedly omitted Negro achievement gained in spite of difficulties; (2) Frazier utilized too many secondary and too few original sources; (3) Frazier's discrediting of cultural survivals among Negroes only reflected "Robert E. Park's lingering dicta that the Negro has retained nothing from the African background"; and (4) other distinguished scholars like Allison Davis, Du Bois, and Carter Woodson understood better than Frazier did that economic or social problems cannot be adequately evaluated with evidence largely from one side. Finally, Brewer concluded that "the bourgeoisie noire [*sic*] is a disservice to Negroes who may be discouraged by the repeated emphasis on dismal failures which rise like Banquo's Ghost at every turn of the torturous routes that American Negroes have had to travel."

In a less damning review of *Black Bourgeoisie,* Maurice Davie noted Frazier's claims of the "myth of the importance of Negro business" and the "exaggeration in the Negro press of the achievements and wealth of Negroes." Davie then "wonders whether the author has not himself indulged in exaggeration." While acknowledging that there is some truth "that some middle-class Negroes try to compensate for their deep feelings of inferiority in a white world" with resulting self-hatred and escape into delusions, Davie accuses Frazier of overstatement and a "lack of adequate substantiation." He states that "little direct evidence is presented concerning the behavior and attitudes of the so-called black bourgeoisie" and then suggests that "perhaps the main basis for the conclusions is personal observation." In other words, Davie is questioning Frazier's sample selection strategy.[5]

August Meier, in a review of *Black Bourgeoisie* in the *Crisis,* agreed that the book presented misleading generalizations, brought about, he said, by Frazier's largely presenting the "subject as an isolated social phenomenon" even though he does recognize that the "behavior" of the black bourgeoisie "is a reflection of American modes

4. *Journal of Negro History* (July 1956): 273–75.
5. *Annals of the American Academy* (July 1957): 167.

of behavior and American values."[6] Meier had hoped for a "more meaningful and better balanced picture." A few of the many problems noted by Meier were (1) Frazier did not really understand the business of the Negro prior to the Civil War and erroneously attributed its emergence to the Freedmen's Bank; (2) Frazier failed to recognize that before World War I occupation and income criteria were as important as family background, education, and conventional behavior in determining social status; (3) Frazier failed to emphasize that the shift of the economic base of Negro business from dependence upon white customers to dependence upon Negro customers had gotten under way by 1900 and been completed during the 1920s (this process, Meier suggested, was related to several developments, including the growing prejudices of whites, the growing spirit of racial self-help and racial solidarity in the face of increasing white hostility, the decline of certain types of small business in which Negroes played an important role, such as draying, catering, and blacksmithing, due to changes in technology and business organization, and the urbanization of Negroes which by 1900 had become significant enough to afford a market that could be exploited by Negro entrepreneurs in banking and insurance); (4) Frazier erred in asserting that the Slater Fund became interested in industrial education due to Booker T. Washington when actually, the Slater Fund was chiefly responsible for creating, during the 1880s, the vogue for industrial education that provided the basis for Washington's fame.

On the other side, Meier supported much of Frazier's sociological analysis, including the charge that members of the black bourgeoisie were chiefly concerned with social life, and conspicuous consumption, and the competitive struggle for status within Negro society. Also, though he admitted that there were exceptions, Meier apparently agreed that there was a characteristic lack of intellectual interest in Negro colleges and interest in the doctorate as a prestige symbol rather than as proof of scholarly achievement, suggesting that social life took precedence over learning. Yet Meier diluted his agreement by suggesting that it was only natural for the Negro elite to imitate the white elite rather than the white liberal professors who disliked empty social striving. Meier went even further and stated that black colleges and white colleges alike often lacked an

6. *Crisis* (Oct. 1957): 461, 469, 517.

intellectual atmosphere. He said Frazier expected too much of human nature and that the striving for status which Frazier abhorred in the black bourgeoisie was also practiced by whites. Meier considered many of Frazier's statements exaggerations and criticized Frazier for suggesting, for example, that the black bourgeoisie despised Africa. Meier stated that the black bourgeoisie had a great interest in Ghana, a fact that undercut Frazier's assumption. He also stated that in criticizing the Negro press, the NAACP, and others, Frazier had underestimated the constructive influences of these groups.

Meier did find some of Frazier's generalizations highly suggestive of further research. He concluded by stating that in spite of his criticisms, *Black Bourgeoisie* was important and said many things that needed saying. The overall negative tone of Meier's review, however, might have persuaded many people not to take a hard look at the volume.

A few less critical reviews also appeared in the same period. Saunders Redding expressed admiration for Frazier and his case selection in the documentation of the self-debasement exhibited by many of the black bourgeoisie. Redding said, the "world of make believe is no prettier or happier than the world of reality. . . . Mr. Frazier's book is a painful documentation of this unhappy thesis."[7]

Barbara Kaplan reviewed *Bourgeoisie Noire* in November 1956; she noted that Frazier's thesis of an inferiority complex among the bourgeoisie drew mainly from psychoanalytic case material reported in *The Mark of Oppression* by Kardiner and Livesy.[8] Readers, she said, were given no data about the number of middle-class Negroes suffering such psychological effects, a matter that backed up her claim that the volume was polemic rather than scientific. Kaplan stated that the book might interest the emerging middle classes in French Africa, thus downplaying the importance of the book for an American audience.

The *American Sociological Review* carried a review of Frazier's *Bourgeoisie Noire* in June 1956 by Everett C. Hughes.[9] It is a rather cool review, containing so few words of praise that one wonders

7. *New York Times Book Review* (Apr. 21, 1957).
8. *American Journal of Sociology* 62, 3 (1956): 335.
9. *American Sociological Review* 21, 3 (1956): 383–84.

how the book won the American Sociological Association's MacIver Lectureship Award.

It is not surprising that black newspapers joined intellectuals in ridiculing Frazier's work since he *had saved his strongest condemnation for them.*

Writing on March 30, 1957, in the *New York Amsterdam News,* Jesse H. Walker notes that while Frazier had won the 1956 MacIver Lectureship Award, he, Walker, doubted that Frazier would receive any award from the black middle class. Walker went on, "I have serious doubts if some of our middle class will ever recover." He notes Frazier's charge that "Negro journalists have been recruited on the whole from the inferior, segregated Negro schools and their outlook has been restricted by the social and mental isolation of the Negro world." Warming to his subject, Walker states that "Greek letter societies, debutante balls and cotillions, the poker playing professions and owners of Cadillacs are sitting ducks on his firing line." Walker ends his review, "It's all rather depressing. Mr. Frazier leaves no hope. What's the use of going on?"[10]

Not to be outdone, George S. Schuyler, columnist for the *Pittsburgh Courier,* calls *Black Bourgeoisie* "a shameless, pamphleteering imposture, venting Leftist spleen under the thin guise of objectivity." Schuyler's review goes downhill after that, and he concludes by stating that "the book should be hailed by Southern politicians, the KKK and the White Citizen's Councils."[11]

What was surprising with regard to the black press's response was that some eight months after Schuyler's review in the *Pittsburgh Courier,* there appeared a very positive review of Frazier's book in the *Courier* by Robert M. Ratcliffe, managing editor. He wrote, "At first you want to tear into Frazier and give him a verbal drubbing for undressing the Negro right out in public. . . . Yet, the more you read what Frazier is saying, the more you realize that his facts are pretty straight." Ratcliffe then indicated that he agreed with Frazier's charges that Negro business was a myth and that "too many Negro teachers refused identification with the Negro masses," and finally that "when Negroes attain middle-class status their lives generally lose both content and significance." Thus, in disagreeing with

10. *New York Amsterdam News* (Mar. 30, 1957), 4.
11. *Pittsburgh Courier* (May 18, 1957).

his colleague Schuyler, Ratcliffe demonstrated that there were some who strongly supported E. Franklin Frazier's views.[12]

Overall, it appears that *Black Bourgeoisie* was not well reviewed when it came out. Indeed, most of the praise from Frazier's academic peers appeared in the scholarly but mixed critique by Meier.

Yet, this is not the whole story, as first appearances are deceiving. What appeared to be rejections of Frazier's charges and/or generalizations are *not denials at all!* Almost unanimously these diverse reviews accept Frazier's charges that the success of Negro businesses is overstated, that the Negro press promulgates the values of the make-believe world of the black bourgeoisie, that the black middle class engages in conspicuous consumption and frivolities, that it suffers from an inferiority complex, and finally, that it has largely ignored the plight of the Negro masses. What the reviews *have* objected to are Frazier's (1) publicizing these matters, or "washing dirty linen" in public, (2) engaging in some exaggeration of the charges, (3) relying on an inadequate sample, and (4) uncritical acceptance of questionable conclusions presented by others. Still most of the reviews presented here accepted the substance of his charges, and some applauded Frazier for his courage in publishing *Black Bourgeoisie.* Finally, it should be emphasized that these observations apply to nearly all the reviewers, whether journalists or academics, black or white.

In the preface to the paperback edition of *Black Bourgeoisie,* published in 1962, Frazier answered his critics. He did not apologize for his position; in fact, he said that many blacks, as well as whites, agreed with his position. Frazier's opinion seems justified.

During the intervening decades, various writers have briefly commented on different aspects of Frazier's *Black Bourgeoisie,* but there does not appear to have been a sustained examination of it since Meier's essay in *Crisis.* G. Franklin Edwards, in a chapter on Frazier in 1974, asserted that the most important element in the book is that it helps one to assess "Frazier's views of what should be the relationship of Negroes to American society." Edwards said that Frazier preferred cultural pluralism over assimilation. Interestingly, just a year earlier, Stanford Lyman had suggested that Frazier, before his untimely death, was apparently on his way to resolving problems

12. Ibid. (Jan. 18, 1958).

blocking the testing of Park's race relations theory, which included assimilation as the final stage.[13]

Later, Wilson J. Moses pointed out that Frazier, as "an avid supporter of integration," was self-contradictory in assaulting the black bourgeoisie's lifestyle.[14]

In sum, subsequent to the early reviews of *Black Bourgeoisie,* there has been a fair amount of interest in the black middle class but with little commentary about Frazier's work. Landry found in his study that, despite claims that the black middle class was growing, it had, in fact, lost ground to whites between 1973 and 1982, and its growth had stopped by 1982. He also noted that middle-class blacks did not live in isolation from the other classes of blacks. Moreover, Landry stated, in sharp disagreement with Frazier, that the black middle class had seemed to shun social clubs by the mid-1970s and instead was involved in mutually beneficial activities in the black community, a change he attributed to the Civil Rights movement. Ross, in a recent volume, has also indicated that the black Greek letter fraternities have been much engaged in national programs designed to benefit black youth and communities since the 1970s. Banks, too, has emphasized that there has been an increased feeling of solidarity among blacks, but that it was brought about by the exclusion of black thinkers from white intellectual institutions.[15]

Cose, in his class analysis, agrees with Frazier that middle-class blacks suffer white insult but suggests that they do not take it lightly; anticipating Banks, Cose says that middle-class blacks suffer high frustration in the Byzantine corporate world, while Banks notes the exclusionary practices of white intellectual institutions.[16]

13. G. Franklin Edwards, "E. Franklin Frazier," in *Black Sociologists: Historical and Contemporary Perspectives,* ed. James Blackwell and Morris Janowitz (Chicago: University of Chicago Press, 1974), 109; Stanford Lyman, *The Black American in Sociological Thought: A Failure of Perspective* (New York: Capricorn Books, 1973), 67.

14. Wilson Jeremiah Moses, *The Wings of Ethiopia: Studies in African-American Life and Letters* (Ames: Iowa State University Press, 1990), 110.

15. Bart Landry, *The New Black Middle Class* (Berkeley: University of California Press, 1987), 193–205; Lawrence C. Ross, *The Divine Nine: The Histories of African American Fraternities and Sororities* (New York: Kensington Books, 2000); William Banks, *Black Intellectuals* (New York: Norton, 1996), 139.

16. Ellis Cose, *The Rage of a Privileged Class* (New York: Harper Collins, 1994); see also James E. Teele, review of *The Rage of a Privileged Class,* by Ellis Cose, *Christian Science Monitor* (Apr. 18, 1994).

All of these writers saw things differently than Frazier. It is quite possible that they saw things differently because things have changed since Frazier wrote *Black Bourgeoisie,* and if things have changed, and middle-class blacks are working on behalf of the black community, then maybe Frazier did, in fact, have some influence on them.

Thus, the lack of a positive initial reception of *Black Bourgeoisie,* the relative inattentiveness to it (and Frazier) in the interim, and the intersection of Frazier's long-ago interests in the black middle class and the black community with current concerns about the black community and middle class argued, it seemed, for a return to *Black Bourgeoisie.* The case for another look at the volume seemed bolstered by the decline, since the 1970s, in a serious discourse on race in America. President William Clinton was probably inspired by this silence to launch his "Initiative on Race."

Moreover, there has been much talk about the growth of the black middle class in recent years. We (the organizers of the symposium) wondered if this were the case and whether Frazier's book could be seen to have played a role in the current circumstances of the black middle class. Thus, we decided to organize a symposium around these issues. We asked participants to develop papers that would focus on issues raised by Frazier in *Black Bourgeoisie* and/or to address the status of the black middle class, past and present. (As indicated in the acknowledgments, we invited other contributors to write for this collection subsequent to the symposium). For this project, we invited academics from the three disciplines in which Frazier had a deep interest: sociology, history, and social work. We did not attempt to bind the individual contributors too tightly to one theme, preferring to give them the freedom to pursue their interests. In only two cases did we request that an author deal with a specific title: Hylan Lewis was asked to focus his paper on Frazier's early days at Howard University, and John Hope Franklin was invited to discuss his personal relationship with Frazier, which began when he was one of Frazier's students at Fisk University. Thus, we included a time dimension in planning the current volume.

This volume focuses on the antecedents, content, style, and conflicts presented by E. Franklin Frazier in *Black Bourgeoisie,* with special attention given to black middle-class dynamics. The present volume does not deal deeply with much of the rest of Frazier's fine tapestry of intellectual production, work that includes research and theory on diverse institutions—family, church, education—as well as on the sociological dynamics of social change and race relations.

The contributors to the present volume have taken on a variety of different tasks in presenting analyses of Frazier's education, research efforts, and motivations as they bear on his assessment of the black middle class. In part one, John Hope Franklin, Hylan Lewis (now deceased), and Adelaide Cromwell present rich and fascinating accounts of their associations with Frazier, focusing primarily on his early and middle years.

In part two, Robert Hall eloquently describes and comments on Frazier's important graduate school experience at the University of Chicago. Hall includes a discussion of Frazier's views on social change before, during, and after his Chicago years. Noting Robert Park's considerable influence on Frazier's academic development, Hall discusses some of the influences on Park's own career, including the influence of Booker T. Washington.

Part three is devoted primarily to a close examination of Frazier's argument about the black middle class. Essays by Anthony Platt, John Bracey, Wornie Reed, Martin Kilson, and Michael Winston make up this section.

Platt, in a wide-ranging piece, focuses on Frazier's academic career (including the fact that no white university made the kind of job offer he merited), on Frazier's claim that too many Negro leaders were opportunistic, and on Frazier's search for agency in the black community. Bracey recounts Frazier's academic experiences, a matter especially interesting and relevant since Bracey came to know Frazier while growing up on Howard's campus. Both Platt and Bracey take up Frazier's ideas about the concept of class with Bracey contributing insight into Frazier's "strange" adaptation of Marxism. Reed examines Frazier's concept of class by focusing on the number of middle-class black males and why this issue matters when considering Frazier's argument in *Black Bourgeoisie.*

While Reed argues that Frazier overestimated the size of the black middle-class male population, Kilson suggests in his essay that Frazier underestimated the size and strengths of the black middle class and its contributions. Furthermore, Kilson argues that Frazier can be criticized on his substantive notion that the black middle class was guilty of excessive and conspicuous consumption. Kilson includes both females and males in his analysis.

In the section's final contribution, Winston focuses on Frazier's global interests, especially his long-term interest in Africa and its connection to his interest in the African American community.[17]

In the conclusion and perspectives section, the editor comments on a couple of recurring themes by contributors, and also on the implication for future research suggested by these contributors. Concluding comments will be brief in recognition of the fact that the authors speak for themselves. It is hoped, however, that this volume represents only the opening stage of a renewal of interest in E. Franklin Frazier's rich and rewarding work.

17. See also Clovis Semmes, "E. F. Frazier on Race and Culture Context: Middle-Class Formation and the Assimilation Problem," paper presented at the spotlight panel cosponsored by the American Sociological Association and the Association of Black Sociologists, Washington, D.C., Aug. 14, 2000.

Part I

Recollections

E. Franklin Frazier

A Memoir

JOHN HOPE FRANKLIN

I first met E. Franklin Frazier at Fisk University in 1931, where I was enrolled in a core course, contemporary civilizations, in which he gave three or four lectures. We freshmen regarded him as a terror, and there were rumors of great rows among the three quite distinguished sociologists on the faculty, Bertram W. Doyle, E. Franklin Frazier, and Charles S. Johnson. We were not certain what the disputes were about or if, indeed, they existed, but they made wonderful gossip, and that was enough for neophytes. Every freshman had his or her favorite sociologist. Some favored Johnson, perhaps because of his quiet dignity and because he was able to dispense considerable funds from the research grants that he always seemed to have. Others favored Doyle because of his quiet folksiness, deep religiosity, and scholarly attainments. Still, there were those who preferred Frazier because of his earthy brusqueness and his indisputable national reputation as a distinguished and productive scholar. All three of them published important books during our undergraduate years. Impressive!

I had almost nothing to say to Frank Frazier until the spring of 1934 as I was ending my junior year at Fisk with a declared major in history. Standing just outside the entrance to the university post office, where both faculty and students inquired about their mail, my classmate asked about my plans for the final summer before graduation. I replied that I did not know if I should take the job offered by Charles Johnson to work with the team he was putting together to study Negro cotton farmers in the South or to go home to Tulsa, Oklahoma, and take my chance for a job there, where I could be with my family. Before my classmate could respond, Frazier joined the conversation and rendered his opinion that it was so typical of undergraduates to be "unable to make up their minds about anything!" I was shocked and embarrassed. On the spot, I declared that I would take the job to work with southern black tenant farmers. It was a memorable summer, and I silently credited Frazier for it. I had no chance to tell him about the summer of 1934, if I had dared, for by the time I returned from my summer job, Frazier had left Fisk to become the chair of the department of sociology at Howard University in Washington, D.C.

I saw little of Frazier until some thirteen years later, when I joined the department of history at Howard University. There had been a few chance encounters in Raleigh, North Carolina, where I was teaching at St. Augustine's College and where Marie Frazier's sister, Julia Delany, wife of a distinguished Raleigh surgeon, also taught. At Howard University, Frazier and I were truly colleagues, holding the same rank of full professor. I was considerably younger, but he genuinely treated me as a colleague in every way, and our frequent association developed into a warm friendship.

One day Frazier asked me if I played poker, and when I replied in the negative, he invited me to join a group of like-minded men on the Howard faculty. The one prerequisite for membership in what was known among its members as the "Thinkers and Drinkers" was that a member did not and would not play poker. The only thing we did was meet, have drinks and dinner, and talk, talk, talk. Frazier was the senior member, joined by two of his colleagues in sociology, Harry Walker and G. Franklin Edwards, and anthropologist Mark Hanna Watkins. There was also a poet, Sterling Brown, a political scientist, Sam Dorsey, an historian, Harold Lewis, and myself.

We met in our respective homes or at our favorite restaurant, Harrisons, on Florida Avenue. None of the members' wives played poker, except Marie Frazier, and I have no doubt that Frazier's antipathy for the game and Marie's devotion to it had something to do with his insisting that no poker player should belong to the "Thinkers and Drinkers." During our meetings, there were no-holds-barred discussions of a variety of social and intellectual topics, but we would invariably end up in a discussion of Howard University and its need to improve its intellectual and educational health. At the end of the meetings, usually held once a month, we felt as though we had solved all or at least most of the problems the various members had introduced.

Frazier derived a certain degree of satisfaction, even pleasure, from the confusion among a few students over Frazier the sociologist and Franklin the historian. Some students were so bewildered that they called us by a garbled name: John Hope Franklin Frazier. One day, I approached Frazier, who had been cornered by a student who insisted that he was John Hope Franklin Frazier. I joined them at Franklin's invitation and was asked to tell the young lady who I was. When I complied, the young lady looked more perplexed than ever as she looked at me, then at him, and then again at me. Suddenly, she seemed to realize, for the first time, that we were two distinctly different people: John Hope Franklin and E. Franklin Frazier.

When Frazier's *The Negro in the United States* was published in 1949, it was a landmark treatise on African Americans from a sociologist's point of view. He approached many problems historically, as was altogether fitting. How else would one approach the changes in, say, the family, housing, or urbanization? Certainly, examining these social systems in the context of change over time was the correct approach. Nevertheless, the work's publication presented me with an excellent opportunity to accuse Frazier of attempting to join the respectable ranks of historians, thus "elevating himself to a new, honorable, and enviable" level of scholarship and esteem. It was after I could no longer conceal my mischief that my friend seemed relieved that I had not gone off the "deep end." After my obviously false and mischievous claims, we agreed that we were, indeed, rivals as historians if not as sociologists.

By the time I had been at Howard for at least five years, Frazier and I were very close friends. Our wives, from the same section of North Carolina, were more than cordial. Even so, my wife, Aurelia, and I were unprepared for their invitation to us to occupy their home for two years while they were in Paris, where Frazier would head the social sciences division of UNESCO. We had been renting an apartment in the far northeast section of the city. When he further specified that our only obligations would be to pay the utility bills and take their mail to his Howard office for forwarding to Paris, we were overwhelmed by this display of thoughtful generosity. Now, not only could I walk to my office from Frazier's nearby

Rhode Island Avenue home, but we could save for a down payment on a home, further facilitated by Aurelia's earning of a master's degree in library science at Catholic University and becoming the librarian at Spingarn High School.

Upon the Fraziers' return from Paris, they greeted us warmly and congratulated us on the birth of our son, who had arrived at the end of our first year in the Frazier home. The only remark made by childless Frazier, who loved children with a passion, was that it was obvious that the huge library he had left in my care was not sufficiently large or challenging enough to take up all of my time. To that remark, I had no rejoinder!

The final comment that Frank Frazier made to me was in 1956, when I accepted the position of chairman and professor in the department of history at Brooklyn College. Above all the din and excitement surrounding the appointment, Frazier called me aside and congratulated me. He went on to say that he was proud of me and delighted that this opportunity had come. Then, this giant of a man, who had reached the pinnacle of his profession and had been president of the American Sociological Society, told me that he would do the same thing if the opportunity arose, but that he was too old. He added prophetically that this would be only the beginning of the move of black scholars to institutions that would "view them not for their color but for what they had to offer." Somehow, I felt better just knowing that in my bidding farewell to Howard University I departed with the blessing of Edward Franklin Frazier.

A Focused Memoir

Howard University and Frazier, 1933–1941

HYLAN A. LEWIS

In this essay I will discuss Howard University just before Frazier's arrival in the 1930s, Frazier's introduction to Washington, D.C., and Howard University and the part I played in his orientation, aspects of his reconstruction of the department of sociology, and the importance of Roosevelt's New Deal. Also of significance is Frazier's standing as an intellectual activist in association with many distinguished colleagues and fellow intellectuals, activists both at Howard and outside the school, in the 1930s and early 1940s. His contemporaries at Howard included Alain Locke, Ralph Bunche, Abram Harris, Edward Lewis, Ernest Just, William Hastie, and James Nabrit.

This cadre of black intellectuals was a significant precursor to today's network of high-profile, public intellectuals, who operate out of somewhat different academic settings, and I'll examine how it functioned and what roles Frazier and other intellectual activists played in it.

The Howard University of this period, marked by the Great Depression and preparation for World War II, used an informal structure. The informal rankings of faculty members in the college of liberal arts and other departments were based largely on conventional formal rankings: professor, associate professor, assistant professor, instructor, and assistant. The informal rankings of administrators was another matter; faculty members tended to present invidious distinctions concerning trappings and prerequisites of administrators' prestige and power.

The informal faculty pyramid comprised three categories: faculty "stars," senior faculty, and junior faculty. Faculty contemporaries were grouped into two relatively rigid, ranked categories:

junior instructors and assistants, most of whom lacked Ph.D.s and tenure, and thus were deferential and expressed insecurities and anxieties in many ways; and professors in senior ranks with tenure and sometimes star status. Members of the latter group were accordingly respected, feared, envied, imitated, and sometimes even slyly mocked by junior faculty members, often with academic "gallows humor."

Aspects of jealous mockery might be seen in some of the nicknames frequently used to categorize tenured, higher-salaried, senior faculty members. One telling label that some used was "plateau boy." And an expression used to slyly designate faculty couples and families who presumably had it made was "they were so well off they ate turkey in the middle of the week."

Frazier automatically belonged to the senior category, but he also came to the university as an academic star—that is, with a reputation based upon scholarly achievements, publications, and ongoing research. The reputation and status of some senior contemporaries were tellingly enhanced for junior faculty if their activities and achievements had included political activism and/or acting as mentors for more junior persons. Frazier had been a rebellious character in the early 1930s; it was said that whites had thrown him out of Atlanta because he was too radical. Therefore, he came to Howard with a reputation as an activist, adding to his star status.

Among Frazier's junior colleagues were several faculty members who more or less straddled the divide between senior and junior colleagues. In this group were Emmett (Sam) Dorsey in political science, William Leo Hansberry in history, John W. Hughley in chemistry, James Porter in art, Frank Snowden in classics, and Doxey Wilkerson in education. With some notable exceptions, junior faculty members tended to exhibit more a rather passive congeniality than an active, overt competitiveness.

Factors that made for across-the-ranks collegiality in the mid-1930s were the organization and functioning of the local chapter of the American Federation of Labor, even though the number of faculty members involved was not large. The organization, changing leadership, and programs of this pioneering faculty union at Howard reflected a conjunction of forces. Initially, the precipitant for a resort to unionism was an acute conflict between a senior faculty member and the president of the university. This happened against a backdrop of long-term dissatisfaction, frustration, and even anger among some senior faculty—much of this directed at the president—and the changing climate of the times, which featured generally aggressive trade union expansion—eventually, if not initially, in part fueled by Marxian and "old left" ideology and politics.

The leadership and membership of the union local included senior professors and teaching assistants. This indicated some across-the-board faculty discontent. Senior professors were among the first leaders of the union. They were followed eventually by union leaders of lower rank who were clearly more to the left ideologically and politically.

Diverse membership in the social science division and in the local union increased interaction between senior and junior faculty; it also increased similarities in some attitudes and sentiments of senior and junior faculty. These similarities in view had to do with the administration, in general, and often with the university's president, in particular. Verbalized dissatisfactions, especially among some senior faculty, affected faculty morale and the institutional climate. The major dissatisfactions seemed to be related to perceptions by many that there were serious gaps between the professions and claims of the university and its institutional performance and productivity. From the time of his arrival in 1935, Frazier played an important role in expressing legitimate faculty discontent.

My participation in the Howard faculty and in the distinctive world of junior colleagues began in the fall of 1933, two years before Frazier came to head and revitalize the department of sociology. Following three quarters of graduate study in the University of Chicago and a job teaching summer school at my alma mater, Virginia Union University, I had received a fellowship from the Social Science Research Council. I joined Abram (Abe) Harris in the economics department as a research assistant in order to do the statistical work on what would later be published as *The Negro as Capitalist*. Interestingly, the fellowship award I received was one designated specifically for southerners. It had been established at the suggestion of Charles S. Johnson, also a graduate of Virginia Union University and one of my undergraduate idols. This award was a precursor of the affirmative action programs in higher education for minorities that would come approximately half a century later. The first three recipients of this award were Estelle Hill from Fisk University, Sarah

Alice Mayfield from Birmingham Southern University, and me, all of whom enrolled in the graduate sociology program at the University of Chicago in the fall of 1932.

The period just before the arrival of Frazier was very significant for the nation, the university, and young academic persons such as myself, and was one of remarkable ferment. Major social, political, and economic changes marked the heady early days of the Roosevelt administration. The New Deal brought significant physical changes to the university: the destruction of the old main building, which had long loomed as the center of the campus, followed by a period of rather quick, dramatic construction. New buildings included the library, Douglass Hall, which housed the classrooms and office into which Frazier moved; the chemistry building, dedicated by President Roosevelt; and three new dormitories—Sojourner Truth, Crandall, and Baldwin—for students and faculty. This growth along with the advent of Mordecai Johnson as the first black president of Howard University made for an exhilarating period at the school. Moreover, Congress favored increased appropriations for Howard. These permitted the university to expand its departments, including liberal arts and, in particular, the professional schools. Behind all of this was support from people like Secretary of the Interior Harold Ickes, Eleanor Roosevelt, and members of the Black Cabinet, as it came to be called; also important were behind-the-scenes efforts that included brokering efforts by Ralph Bunche in relationship to Howard University and the administration.[1] The university had reached a turning point.

Amidst all this activity, Frazier arrived. At first he lived, as did many faculty members in the early days, in one of the new dormitories because specific housing for the faculty was not available. So,

1. President Roosevelt was said to rely on the Black Cabinet, an informal advisory group made up of distinguished African Americans, when making decisions pertinent to black Americans. In 1938, the group included Ambrose Caliver, Roscoe Brown, Robert C. Weaver, Joseph H. Evans, Frank Horne, Mary McLeod Bethune, Lawrence D. Oxley, William J. Thompkins, Charles E. Hall, William J. Houston, Ralph E. Mizelle, Dewer R. Jones, Edgar Brown, J. Parker Prescott, Edward H. Lawson, Arthur Weiseger, Alfred Edgar Smith, Henry A. Hunt, John W. Whitten, and Joseph R. Houchins. At other times William H. Hastie, Eugene Kinkle Jones, and William Trent were included. Langston Hughes and Milton Meltzer, *A Pictorial History of the Negro* (New York: Crown Publishers, 1963), 285.

he and his wife, Marie, lived in Sojourner Truth Hall, along with students and other members of the faculty and staff. Soon after the Fraziers' arrival, arrangements were made for them to occupy a house on northwest Rhode Island Avenue, which was just turning from white occupancy to Negro occupancy. The Fraziers moved out of Sojourner Truth Hall and into 220 Northwest Rhode Island Avenue. At the time, I was working as an assistant in the economic department and living in Sojourner Truth Hall. I was close to the Fraziers and helped them move to their new house. I stayed with Mrs. Frazier while her husband tied things up at Fisk University, then I left the Fraziers' household to marry a Howard graduate student, Leighla Whipper.

One of the important tasks set for Frazier by the university was the revitalization of the sociology department. This was part of a general effort to enhance the quality of staffing in all the departments and professional schools at Howard. At the time Frazier left Fisk University, and his association with Charles S. Johnson in the social science department, Howard's sociology department was staffed by people who were not involved in modern developments in sociology. The department included Kelly Miller, who was about to retire, and Gold Refined Wilson, who had been at the University of Chicago and who was known for his flamboyant style and his racy automobiles. He had a rather mysterious—if not romantic—background, related to his experiences in Latin America (especially Haiti), and junior faculty regarded him as a real character who loved long cars and women. He had a long scar on his cheek. Legend held that while doing fieldwork on voodoo in Haiti, he had stuck his head into a tent when a voodoo service was going on and been struck by a machete. The sociology department also included Henderson Donald, a Yale Ph.D. and somewhat of a loner with a reputation as an ineffective teacher and lecturer.

Frazier was brought in to overhaul the department. One of the things he did was encourage Henderson Donald to resign. Donald was quite stubborn about leaving. Frazier began to ask him about his sociological interests and credentials. He once asked him about his activities in the American Sociological Association. Frazier said, "Well, for example, how many conventions have you gone to in the last few years?" And Donald said, "Well, I really haven't been to any, I haven't had enough money to go." And Frazier responded,

"Dr. Donald, do you know that the American Sociological Association met last year in Washington, D.C.!" Donald eventually retired.

I transferred from the department of economics to sociology and took over many of the courses Donald had taught. In 1935 I became an assistant in sociology. Gold Refined Wilson and Kelly Miller also left, and the department consisted of Frazier, W. O. Brown, and me.[2] Later, Haridas Mazumdar joined the faculty, and Samuel Strong and Harry Walker were eventually brought in to teach when either Frazier or I was on leave. Supporting staff included secretaries Mrs. Leora Hadley, and Zulma (Nuffie) McNeil (who later married Cab Calloway). Another significant figure in the department was Dennis Nelson, a graduate student and research assistant in the sociology laboratory. Nelson was later recruited out of Howard and became one of the first Negro naval officers.

Since I had been around Howard University for two or three years, I was able to help Frazier with his introduction and orientation. Among the first things that I did was to tell him about some monies which were available to faculty for scholarly efforts and travel. This came at a time when he was interested in going to the social work convention in Atlantic City. From those funds, he was able to get enough money—fifty to one hundred dollars—to make the trip, and he took me along with him. We drove to Atlantic City in his little red coupe with the rumble seat. I will never forget that as we took I-40 through Baltimore, Frazier suddenly detoured by an old market. Sounding like a little boy, he said, "I want to stop here." He went into the market and searched for a little candy stall; when he found it, he joyfully bought some peanut brittle. This was the same stall where he had bought peanut brittle when he was a very young man in Baltimore. We munched peanut brittle all the way to Atlantic City. On that trip, I was struck by how many of the social work people, particularly the black ones, flocked around Frazier, almost as though he were a rock star. Of course, this *was* "Dr. Frazier." He was a star both to the social workers and the sociologists.

In the first or second year, Frazier decided to establish a curriculum in social work. He and I taught together the first course in

2. William O. Brown, a white Texan, later left Howard University for a position in the State Department, where he remained until 1953, when he became the first director of the African Studies Program at Boston University.

the social work curriculum, which was on social research. The first person recruited for the program was Ruth Jackson, who was from the University of Chicago School of Social Work. Later, the dedicated curriculum evolved into a full-fledged professional school of social work with Annabelle Lindsey as its first director.

Frazier's interest and energy were crucial to giving vitality to and gaining recognition for the sociology department. One of his first steps was to start a sociology laboratory modeled after that of the University of Chicago and geared to urban studies and the creative use of census tract data. Frazier was responsible for keeping the department staffed while he or others were on leave, whether he was in Harlem studying the causes of the 1937 race riot at the invitation of mayor La Guardia or filling in for me while I completed my graduate work at the University of Chicago.

Frazier's connection to the University of Chicago began with his early days in the Atlanta School of Social Work. It was then that he met Robert Park. Park became one of Frazier's early mentors, and until Park died, he continued to play a significant role in Frazier's scholarly and academic activities.[3] At Chicago Frazier was influenced by Park in terms of his theoretical and perceptual framework. Two other people—E. W. Burgess and Louis Wirth—also figured very prominently in his scholarly and academic career. This linkage with Chicago not only was important in defining Frazier, himself, but also in affecting the recruiting and the appointment of staff at Howard. W. O. Brown, Samuel Strong, G. Franklin Edwards, Harry Walker, and I were all from Chicago. Only Haridas Mazumdar was from someplace else—Wisconsin. Horace Fithcit, also derivative of Chicago, taught at Claflin University in South Carolina. Frazier always wanted to bring him to Howard but was never successful. Frazier maintained an especially strong link to those who were Chicago graduates, Chicago-oriented, or had shared experiences with him at Fisk. His main educational reference groups and intellectual reference points were Chicago and Fisk.

Frazier's achievements and contributions to change and scholarship during the New Deal occurred at a time when Howard University was a major institutional force. The university had gone through

3. Ernest W. Burgess, Robert Park, Ellsworth Faris, William F. Ogburn, W. I. Thomas, and Louis Wirth were key figures in the University of Chicago's sociology department during Frazier's time.

a physical and spiritual transformation. New buildings, a strengthening of its professional schools, and the vital additional contribution of some significant campus figures helped give birth to a new sense of academic maturity and growth for the university.

The state of higher education for Negroes in America and new vistas for the changing Negro community need to be judged in this context. Frazier and many of his friends were people of stature. The prewar convergence of confluences at Howard University served as a major "in gathering," sharpening the university's focus and highlighting emergent trends. Frazier, and others, gave significant meaning to identity politics among Negroes both in and outside of the academic world. In many ways these figures reflected an interrelatedness of American intellectual and political affairs.

These men and women gave accent and much wider range to what had been a relatively limited and parochial attitude toward prewar Negro affairs and perspectives. Much of this was an outgrowth of changing relationships within the academic community. Frazier and many of his academic colleagues were leaders of a kind of intellectual crossover. Even though they sometimes were victims of a rather vicious segregation and discrimination, they did not cry out for themselves but fought strenuously and courageously, and frequently prevailed, in spite of the racial climate. Much of this crossover had to do not only with the academics, but also with the interrelationship of race and labor. This was a very important synthesis for Frazier in the 1920s and 1930s. Frazier especially symbolized a meaningful combination of the values of race, science, politics, and Americanism. He helped facilitate a changing Negro identity in America. During this period, engagements of the Negro intellectuals with "white Marxism" were often degrading and sometimes threatening; however, these dynamics always influenced, in some measure, aspects of politics and ideology. It is only fair to remember that Frazier and others dealt with these political forces despite the pressures and changing orientations that were characteristic of this important time.

I wish to emphasize that Frazier was a gladiator in the fullest sense of the word; however, he eschewed the often accompanying role of clown. The many battles he fought—in places like Atlanta, Nashville, and Washington—prove my claim. Frazier strongly encouraged sociologists to choose important topics to study and then choose or devise appropriate methodologies, not the other way around. Similarly, he would urge his students, and black leaders, to confront issues that were important to the black community. Such concerns probably played a part in his later decision to write *Black Bourgeoisie*.

Frazier's Background and an Overview

ADELAIDE M. CROMWELL

In assessing works by black novelists and poets, scholars often expect that these works will reveal, indeed be based on, the lives and personal values of the authors—even if they are not autobiographical by design. But it is quite another matter when we attempt to evaluate the contributions of black social scientists whose main theses are usually determined by studying how the black community or a significant portion of that community is affected by its contact with the larger society. The assumption is always that by using the appropriate methodology the black social scientist can objectively study his own community, perhaps with more sensitivity but always with the detachment of a scholar. I have no quarrel with this expectation.

However, Harold Cruse reminds us that

> the peculiarities of the American social structure, and the position of the intellectual class within it, make the functional role of the Negro intellectual a special one. The Negro intellectual must deal intimately with the white power structure and cultural apparatus, and the inner realities of the black world at one and the same time . . . he has to be acutely aware of the nature of the American social dynamic and how it monitors the ingredients of class stratification in American society.[1]

Obviously not all intellectuals are social scientists, but all social scientists should be intellectuals. And on that basis, Cruse's caution is worth noting.

I am not aware of any prominent black social scientist who has offered student readers some insight into how or why he or she identifies with a given subject. Surely, it would be instructive to know

1. Harold Cruse, *The Crisis of the Negro Intellectual* (New York: William Morrow, 1987), 451.

how the interest emerged as well as the marital status of a scholar writing on the family or if a scholar who studied and reported on crime, gangs, and delinquency had a criminal history.

E. Franklin Frazier, unfortunately, wrote no autobiography, so it is difficult to know why he selected certain topics for study. However, Frazier did grant an interview to James Moss, which Frazier corrected when transcribed, thus adding to its veracity.[2] Information in that interview and knowledge gained from my own long friendship with Frazier, who was never shy about expressing his views on any subject, form the basis of this essay.

My friendship with Frazier began when he solicited my cooperation as a subject for his book *Negro Youth at the Crossways*.[3] I am not sure how he identified me, but at that time in Washington, D.C., the names of students attending Ivy League colleges were fairly well known. On the basis of this contact, the following year, in 1939, as president of the sociology club of Smith College, I invited Frazier to give a lecture. His willingness to come was no doubt influenced by the fact that Frank Hankins, then a professor at Smith, had been his professor and mentor when Hankins taught at Clark. From then on, Frazier took an interest in my career, first as a sociologist and later as an Africanist. In 1962, the year he died, Frazier invited me to give a lecture on *Social Work in Africa* to his class at Howard University.

E. Franklin Frazier was born in Baltimore, Maryland, on September 24, 1894, one of five children of James H. Frazier, a bank messenger, and Mary Clark Frazier, a housewife. Thus, his family was not a part of the flourishing black bourgeoisie of Baltimore, which was made up of lawyers, doctors, teachers, and businessmen. He attended Baltimore public schools then went on to Howard University from which he graduated with honors in 1916. Frazier began his long teaching career at black institutions: Tuskegee (mathematics, 1916–1917), St. Paul's Normal and Industrial School in Lawrenceville, Virginia (English and history, 1917–1918), and Baltimore High School (French and mathematics, 1918–1919). At none of these schools, perhaps, would he have been exposed quickly to the black middle class,

2. James Moss is deceased, and the notes on the interview have been destroyed.

3. E. Franklin Frazier, *Negro Youth at the Crossways: Their Personality Development in the Middle States* (Washington, D.C.: American Council on Education, 1940).

and the brevity of his appointments probably would have discouraged him from seeking it out.

Frazier's interest in a teaching career apparently was the result of his exposure to two individuals: W. E. B. Du Bois and an unnamed high school teacher who "though not a great scholar, enjoyed books and had a great respect for learning."

Though he might not at that point have actually met Du Bois, Frazier was certainly aware of his scholarship and activism. He expressed that admiration during the bitter period of the cold war by presiding at a dinner in New York in honor of Du Bois. It took courage; many of Du Bois's so-called friends and admirers, frightened by the political risks, refused to attend.

I do not know how Frazier secured his first teaching position or how and why he made his first venture out of and away from the black world to pursue graduate education at a white institution, Clark University in Worcester, Massachusetts. There he was introduced to sociology as a formal discipline. In 1920 he received his master's degree. The topic of his thesis was *New Currents of Thought among the Colored People of America*. At Clark, as I have mentioned, Hankins was his mentor. According to G. Franklin Edwards, a colleague of Frazier's at Howard University, Frazier frequently mentioned that "it was during his year at Clark that his career as a sociologist began and that the year of study with Hankins had a profound effect upon his intellectual development though he did not always agree with Hankins's position on race and other social problems."[4] This is not surprising since, in addition to a basic sociology text, Hankins wrote *The Racial Basis of Civilization*. However, as another of Hankins's students, I could vouch for the fact that his theories never hindered his encouragement of nor interest in black students.

After spending a year (1920–1921) as a Russell Sage Foundation fellow at the New York School of Social Work (later Columbia University School of Social Work) and a year at the University of Copenhagen, where he studied folk high schools, as a fellow of the American Scandinavian Foundation, Frazier returned to the black world in 1922, accepting an appointment at Atlanta University.

4. Frank H. Hankins, *An Introduction to the Study of Society*, rev. ed. (New York: Macmillan, 1935).

There he was director of the Atlanta School of Social Work and an instructor of sociology at Morehouse College.

It was at this point, I believe, that Frazier first met the black middle class and observed the constraints put upon it by the larger society. One of his early essays, "Durham: Capital of the Black Middle Class," published in *The New Negro: An Interpretation,* extolled the virtues of the Negro businessman of Durham, whom he described as a mixture of peasant and gentleman.[5] During his first year at Morehouse, Frazier married Marie Brown of Winston, North Carolina. She was a large, light-skinned woman who enjoyed poetry and painting and came from a middle-class background. Her father, Calving Scott Brown, was a minister and educator. He established Waters Normal Institute in Winston, North Carolina. Her mother, Ameza Drummond Brown, was thought to be the descendant of the first governor of the state. It was at this point that Frazier began experiencing disappointment in black institutions of education—first with the students:

> I think the most disturbing aspect of my teaching in a Negro college is this great indifference on the part of the students to learning anything. Of course, that is the influence of American culture generally. It is also the influence of the Negro community and the Negro newspapers also. Most of the teachers in the schools to whom I've taught have had the same experience. They resist the resistance on the part of the Negro students to learn anything.

During this period, Frazier published a number of articles on the African American family, the cooperative movement, business enterprise among African Americans, and the role of social work among African Americans. His article "The Pathology of Race Prejudice" elicited such strong reactions among whites in Atlanta that Frazier was fired from his position.[6] He was fired for daring to advocate racial equality; he insisted that African Americans should not attend affairs where they were to be segregated. Of course, he was addressing his remarks to his social work students, but the article went further. In sum, his hypothesis was that racial prejudice was

5. Alain Locke, ed., *The New Negro: An Interpretation* (New York: Albert & Charles Boni, 1925), 333–40.

6. E. Franklin Frazier, "The Pathology of Race Prejudice," *Forum* 70 (June 1927): 856–62.

analogous to insanity. He reasoned that the prejudiced person, in maintaining the basis of his prejudice, resorted to the same rationalization that an insane person would in explaining his definition of a situation. Such behavior, Frazier called the "Negro Complex," and he said that the Negro Complex and the attitudes associated with it affected the behavior of whites on a variety of unrelated subjects. He described its manifestation by using many examples from the racial etiquette of the South as applied to Negroes.

Frazier indicated that when this article appeared in the *Atlanta Constitution,* with incorrect implications, on June 10, 1927, a special meeting of the board of the school of social work was called, and both the black and white members decided that he had to go. Frazier felt that the liberal whites only pretended to be advocates of blacks and did not want to face them as equals—or even near-equals. Afterward, Frazier said, an edict went out that he should never again be allowed to teach in a black school.

As my father used to say about the use of such tactics, Frazier was blackballed. And the boards of the many white-supported black schools were then, if not now, part of a larger network through which such information could be easily and quickly disseminated. Having defined the parameters of southern society from the outside in, Frazier was run out of town.

Fortunately, he was rescued by the University of Chicago's sociology department, which was, he remembered, "acquainted with what I intended to do in the field of sociology," and offered a research assistantship. He later said about the university, "I will always have a deep and abiding affection for the University of Chicago because at the critical period in my life the University of Chicago was the only institution that came forth to offer me an opportunity to continue my career in the field of sociology."

Frazier and his wife, Marie, were exposed to the black life of Chicago—to Bronzeville, as St. Clair Drake and Horace Cayton called it in *Black Metropolis.*[7] Chicago had, at the time, the second largest black community in the world, exceeded only by Harlem. It was a city within a city.

In his introduction to *Black Metropolis,* Richard Wright described Chicago as

7. St. Clair Drake and Horace R. Cayton, *Black Metropolis: A Study of Negro Life in a Northern City* (New York: Harcourt Brace, 1945).

> the city from which the most incisive and radical Negro thought has come, there is an open and raw beauty about that city that seems to fill or endow one with the spirit of life . . . *Black Metropolis* reveals 1) the relationship of Negroes to Whites in Chicago, 2) the kind of world which Negroes have built up under their separate, subordinate status, and 3) the impact of these twin configurations upon the personalities and institutions of Chicago Negroes.[8]

Later in the book Drake and Cayton describe what they call an upper class:

> a small group of actually wealthy Negroes—had also several hundred families, which even during the Depression, received incomes from $5000 to $15,000 a year. This category included professionals, businessmen and higher civil servants. . . . This group, middle class by general American standards, forms the core of Bronzeville's upper class . . . it jealously guards its social status, stressing "culture," "refinement" and "education" and erecting social barriers against the "upper shadies"—the very wealthy who have gained their wealth through the rackets. The upper class admits to its circles many whose incomes are far less than theirs but who possess other valued attributes, such as advanced education or high standards of public decorum.[9]

Just imagine the effect the exposure to Chicago had on the young Frazier and his wife. They had never seen anything like it. Doctors were on the faculty of the white medical schools, and teachers taught in an integrated system. Moreover, Frazier met people like Earl Dickerson, an attorney who helped the career of John Johnson of *Ebony* and *Jet;* Robert Abbott of the *Chicago Defender;* Jesse Binga, the banker; and Claude Barnett of the Negro Press Associates. I remember visiting Chicago as a child and being struck by the vibrancy and apparent wealth of the black elite community.

If this was visible to me as a child, how much more it would have meant to Frazier, who knew only Baltimore, Washington, D.C., Atlanta, and Durham! It is worth noting that Chicago had a powerful group of racketeers, linked to a comparable group in the larger society, and it was a community that had the vote and, therefore, political power. Any games within the black group really had to be played out on a larger board. It was the Chicago electorate that in 1928 sent

8. Ibid., xvii–xix.
9. Ibid., 514–15.

the first post-Reconstruction black Congressman, Oscar DePriest, to Washington, D.C.

Fortuitously, Frazier was being welcomed into a sociology department that expected its students to go forth and study the community. Its reputation as the "Chicago School" led by such giants in the field as Robert Park, Ernest Burgess, and Ellsworth Faris who stressed the combined methods of quantitative research and case histories for all of their students who ultimately published some thirteen dissertations based on these methods. Frazier's *The Negro Family in Chicago* and Louis Wirth's *The Ghetto* are among the most noteworthy. Frazier later applied the methods he had used in his dissertation to two larger books, *The Negro Family in the United States* and *The Negro Youth at the Crossways,* part of a research study sponsored by the American Council on Education on the effect of prejudice on black youth in various geographical regions. All the works reveal his exploration of social stratification in the black community; each environment he studied sharpened his awareness of the differences among them.[10]

Frazier was so much a part of the academic establishment of the University of Chicago that Oliver Cromwell Cox, a contemporary, felt that he "had promoted his career through compromise with the sociological establishment. Cox wrote that "one can discern most clearly the hand of Park on the intellectual life of Frazier. . . . His professional career had to be contrived on the tightrope set up by the associational establishment."[11] Frazier's position at the university afforded him access to the black elite of Chicago. Years later, Frazier said, "There was a period for instance, after getting my Ph.D.

10. E. Franklin Frazier, *The Negro Family in Chicago* (Chicago: University of Chicago Press, 1932); Louis Wirth, *The Ghetto* (Chicago: University of Chicago Press, 1928); E. Franklin Frazier, *The Negro Family in the United States* (Chicago: University of Chicago, 1932); Frazier, *Negro Youth.*

11. Oliver Cromwell Cox (1901–1974), a Marxist sociologist, received a Ph.D. in sociology from the University of Chicago in 1938. While interested in race relations, Cox, a West Indian, constantly criticized the works of southerners Johnson and Frazier. His publications include a trilogy on capitalism: *The Foundations of Capitalism* (1959), *Capitalism and American Leadership* (1962), and *Capitalism as a System* (1964). Despite his credentials, Cox, like Frazier, was denied an opportunity to teach at the University of Chicago and had to seek employment in black colleges. In 1970, after he had retired from regular teaching, he accepted a post as distinguished visiting professor of sociology at Wayne State. See Herbert M. Hunter and Sameer Y. Abraham, eds., *Race, Class, and the World System: The Sociology of Oliver C. Cox* (New York: Monthly Review Press, 1987), xxxvi–xxxvii.

at Chicago in 1931, when I could have stayed on that staff, and I would have been worked right up to a professor. I know that from what happened later." And yet in the same interview he remarks, "Yes, I would say now when I was at the University of Chicago and came out . . . I knew the only place I would find a job was in a Negro college. At that time it was the only place I expected to find one." E. Franklin Frazier was a realist.

Whatever the reality, Frazier did go from the university to a black college—Fisk. He was at Fisk but not of Fisk because "You see, the shadows were still over me as being a radical Negro, believing in racial equality. So I carried my own salary there and began my work on *The Negro Family in the United States.* I stayed at Fisk University five years . . . for the first two years I was paid out of a grant given me by the Social Science Research Council. The last three years I was paid by Fisk University."

At this time, Frazier's interest was increasingly focused on stratification within the black community, with as much attention given the upper or middle strata as the lower strata, and the black family, and so intertwined were the two that it is difficult to ascertain which had for him the greater priority. However, it is abundantly clear that Frazier's exposure to the Chicago scene was critical to his understanding of both the black family and the black upper class.

During this period, Frazier published "Certain Aspects of Conflict in the Negro Family."[12] He saw family conflicts emerging because the black family lacked well-defined social and economic classes with established traditions, yet, at the same time, differences in color and complexion determined social status and development of personality among blacks. He saw that the composition of the black elite class varied according to the size, general culture, and history of the black community and was not based on occupational differentiation.

While at Fisk, Frazier continued his examination of the fortunate or advantaged blacks relative to their brethren in *The Free Negro Family* (1932), again discussing both the characteristics of the free Negro community and those of individual families surviving within it.[13] He

12. E. Franklin Frazier, "Certain Aspects of Conflict in the Negro Family," *Social Forces* (Oct. 1931).

13. E. Franklin Frazier, *The Free Negro Family* (Nashville, Tenn.: Fisk University Press, 1932).

dedicated the book to his wife's parents, Calving Scott and Ameza Drummond Brown.

Frazier was not happy at Fisk. His comments suggest that he was beginning to reexamine the environment of the black college into which he had never comfortably fit. Frazier never said why he left Fisk. Apparently, his study at Chicago and performance at Fisk had removed the stigma of his dismissal in Atlanta. A position at Howard University, which was located in the more stimulating environment of Washington, D.C., would certainly have appealed. Nashville would have seemed dull and restrictive compared with Chicago. There may have been a certain incompatibility with Charles S. Johnson (1893–1956), an important member of the Fisk faculty who later became the university's president. Both men had been students of Robert Park's and were ostensibly seeking the same academic achievement, but Frazier was awarded a Ph.D. degree in 1931 and Johnson was awarded a Ph.B. in 1918 but never received a Ph.D. Johnson, however, proved to be both a scholar and an administrator. In addition to serving as editor of *Opportunity,* the National Urban League's magazine, Johnson wrote or cowrote some seventeen books. His best known were *The Negro in Chicago, Shadow of the Plantation, The Negro in American Civilization, Growing up in the Black Belt* and *Patterns of Negro Segregation.*[14]

Today, one is tempted to imagine the actual relations between Frazier and Johnson and Frazier and Cox. They were all outstanding scholars but of different temperaments and caught in an academic environment barely accepting of black scholars—even the University of Chicago, probably the most liberal among outstanding universities of the day. Indeed it was the University of Chicago that later offered a post in education to Allison Davis, probably a first academic post in a white university.[15] One wonders how Park really felt about these three outstanding men. Did he evaluate them

14. See also Richard Robbins, *Sideline Activist: Charles S. Johnson and the Struggle for Civil Rights* (Jackson: University of Mississippi Press, 1996), 65, 78–79, 181–82, for an interpretation of the Frazier-Johnson relationship.

15. Allison Davis (1902–1983), a cultural anthropologist, received an AB from Williams College and a Ph.D. from the University of Chicago; he was a research associate at Harvard University before being appointed to the faculty at the University of Chicago. He was the author of *Children of Bondage* (1940) and *Cultural Deprivation* (1964).

differently? In any case, none was offered a faculty position. So Frazier and Johnson left for Fisk, and Cox left for Wiley College in Texas.

While at Fisk, Frazier was still trying to understand the problem of class in the black community as exemplified in black colleges. He told Moss that there

> you had what you have today in many Negro colleges. Many Negro colleges . . . cater to a new Negro middle class, and you had the heart of that at Fisk University. . . . I remember one girl had a nervous breakdown because her father was a skilled mechanic in Gary, Indiana and the girls would sit around and talk about their mothers' mink coats, their fine cars and so forth. She told me she felt like going through the floor. Now that sort of thing was typical of Negro Colleges.

Frazier, in his stories to Moss, was less cordial in his recall of Fisk than of Chicago.

> I have always been underpaid, if I compare my salary with Negro administrators on one hand, or with my white colleagues on the other hand . . . When I went to Fisk I received $1,000.00 less than the so-called distinguished professors there, none of whom had any distinction at all. It was simply on the basis of bargaining. When I left Fisk and came to Howard, I received a salary less than certain other professors received. In a school like Howard, the administrators received the high salaries no matter what their distinction may be.

In any case, in 1934 Frazier left Fisk for Howard University, where he was to be chairman of the sociology department. The black community, however, fed on itself in a way it did not in Chicago—despite its members' interest in education—because Washington was a strictly segregated society. The black elite had talent, money, and education but no voting power, so there was no political vehicle for change.

Frazier never did a serious or, shall we say, empirical study of the black community of Washington. It was to be home to him and his wife, Marie, for the rest of his life. And though she could be critical of it, she thoroughly adjusted to it. Her brother even moved to Washington, married into an old family, and opened a medical practice in the city. He and his wife lived across the street from the Fraziers.

The Fraziers eventually built a summer home at Highland Beach, a resort for blacks near Annapolis, Maryland, which, while started by the sons of Frederick Douglass, quickly became the place where only the "right" people had homes, and the beach was restricted to residents and their guests. The Fraziers had become members of the elite. During the couple's many happy summers there Frazier often read or wrote.

While at Howard, Frazier also undertook some additional and interesting responsibilities. From 1935 through 1936, he was the director of a commission that investigated the social and economic conditions responsible for the Harlem riot of March 19, 1935. The assignment lasted for the one year, but the commission's report was never published.

Ten years later the Armstrong-Hemingway Foundation of Boston invited Frazier to undertake a survey of race relations in Boston. Accordingly, he submitted a memorandum in which, among other points to be examined, was a study of the class structure of the black community, which Frazier stated was important in any fundamental study of race relations. The study he envisaged was to take six months; he would be the director with an assistant, clerical staff, and field workers (some of whom would be students). Estimated cost for the project fifteen thousand dollars. The study was not done. It is not surprising. Going forward with the study, or allowing the commission's report to be published, would have required implementation for which neither community was prepared.

In 1941, long before the Armstrong-Hemingway Foundation approached him and soon after completing *Negro Youth at the Crossways,* Frazier received a Guggenheim Fellowship to study the structure of family life in Brazil. Upon his return a year later, Frazier's next important academic activity was assisting Gunner Myrdal, a Swedish economist hired in 1938 by Carnegie to direct the largest ever research project on race relations. Six years later, its results were published as the now well-known book *An American Dilemma.*[16] In the book's earliest phase Frazier prepared a memorandum on recreation, which was ultimately reduced to a few pages in the final report. Later however Frazier and Louis Wirth were asked to critique

16. Gunner Myrdal, Richard Sterner, and Arnold Rose, *An American Dilemma: The Negro Problem and Modern Democracy* (New York: Harper & Brothers, 1944).

the completed manuscript. Frazier completed his highly laudatory appraisal in fifteen days. From 1951 through 1953 he served as director of the Division of Applied Social Sciences of the United Nations Educational, Scientific, and Cultural Organization in Paris. During this period Frazier lectured at the University of London, the University of Edinburgh and the University of Liverpool. Around the same time he gave the lecture that would be published (in its English version) as *Black Bourgeoisie*.[17]

It is for this book that Frazier is largely remembered, although I don't think he would like that. In writing *The Black Bourgeoisie* while in France, away from the scene, as it were, Frazier might have felt freer to express observations that he either had been unwilling or unable to verify empirically. The book's main thesis is that the black bourgeoisie was made up not of merchants, as in most middle classes, but of persons in professional and clerical positions. The rapid social rise of this group drew attention to the material goods its members had acquired and their imitation of upper-class values. However, the group lacked a substantive basis for much of this behavior; in fact, with no interest in education or the arts and without the moral ethics of older middle classes, they lived in a world of make-believe. Clearly, Frazier had observed this sort of behavior, particularly in Washington. What it would take to break these barriers or, as Cruse had noted, deal intimately with the white power structure, Frazier does not address.

During the last twenty years of his life, especially after his return from France, Frazier seemed to become obsessed by the repressive environment of black colleges, especially that of Howard University. He was at Howard during the rise and heyday of Mordecai Johnson, a Baptist minister and the first black president of the university. Frazier said of Johnson and his administration,

> Howard University administration is an autocratic one—nobody pays any attention to the teachers around here. The Dean came into the faculty not long ago and said that the administrative had decided to let us contribute to the educational policy of the university. This was a great innovation—that teachers were going to contribute to the education! Even though I am a full professor here, no administrator

17. E. Franklin Frazier, *Bourgeoisie Noire* (Paris: Plon, 1955); *Black Bourgeoisie* (New York: Free Press, 1957).

> would show the same respect for my opinion as was shown at the University of Chicago, though I was only a research assistant. What is important in the Negro school is status, not education and that is the reason a lot of them are resisting integration because they are afraid of losing power and status.

Frazier did not hesitate to discuss his views of Johnson with others. He had mixed feelings about the opportunities for black professors at white colleges despite his assertion that he could have stayed at the University of Chicago. He said that there were as many Negroes teaching in white colleges as could be expected: "I don't believe that there are many competent teachers unemployed because of discrimination in New York Colleges. . . . I think if a young Negro goes about it the right way he can get a job in a white college."

For all his accomplishments, Frazier's career ended on rather a sad note. He was invited to teach an occasional course here and there—at Sarah Lawrence, the New York School of Social Work, the University of California at Berkeley, and Carlton College—but he was not offered a position commensurate with his status, and when other black scholars (Abram Harris, Ralph Bunche, Doxey Wilkerson, and Ernest Just to name only a few) abandoned Howard University, Frazier, like Sterling Brown, stayed on. Unlike Brown, he did not live long enough to be rediscovered. The positions offered him were beneath him—and he gradually saw that—and that is how I got my first teaching position. Hunter College wrote him about a part-time "great opportunity" in 1942, I believe. He had the good judgment not to take it but was kind enough to recommend me, a junior scholar whom he himself described as an "embryonic" sociologist in my copy of *The Negro Family in the United States.*

Frazier did receive a number of honors, however. He was the first African American to be elected president of a professional association—the American Sociological Society (1948). He was also elected president of the African Studies Association, but he did not live to serve. He had been a founding member and later president of the District of Columbia Sociological Society (1943–1944) and the Eastern Sociological Society (1944–1945).

I have not discussed Frazier's political views because, frankly, they were not a part of our discussions. G. Franklin Edwards notes that St. Clair Drake refers to Frazier as a neo-Marxist, and Bessie Delaney, in the delightful *Having Our Say,* recalls incidents of Frazier's participation, along with Du Bois and Walter White, in the New York boycott of *The Birth of a Nation.*[18] But our talks revealed only his forthrightness and uncompromising positions on racial equality and on the repressive environment of black colleges.

Some scholars will attribute his cutting analysis of the black bourgeoisie to his earlier socialist inclinations, but I believe his indictment of the black bourgeoisie targeted not the class itself but rather the lost opportunities and lack of involvement in the issues of importance to blacks. This he deplored. I wonder what Frazier would have written if he had been offered a position at the University of Chicago and could have observed how that community used its political power. While I was never his student, I believe we learned much from each other.

18. G. Franklin Edwards, ed., *E. Franklin Frazier on Race Relations* (Chicago: University of Chicago Press, 1968); Sarah Delaney, Elizabeth Delaney, and Amy Hill Hearth, *Having Our Say: The Delaney Sisters' First One Hundred Years* (New York: Kodansha International, 1933), 137–39.

Part II

Graduate Study

E. Franklin Frazier and the Chicago School of Sociology

A Study in the Sociology of Knowledge

ROBERT L. HALL

Edward Franklin Frazier has been damned and praised with equal vigor from many quarters. Two Chicago-trained black sociologists, Oliver Cromwell Cox and Abdul Ibn Alkalimat (Gerald McWorter) have published biting criticisms of the "pernicious influences" of Frazier's Chicago mentors. Frazier's theories and research are far from dead; Daniel Patrick Moynihan claimed merely to be extending and documenting his notions about the social disorganization of urban black communities.[1] A study of the sociology of Frazier's knowledge about race relations should be a valuable contribution to the continuing debate over social influences on race-relations scholarship. This essay is divided into three broad topics: Robert E. Park, the Chicago School of Sociology, and E. Franklin Frazier. In the first section, Park's career line is traced with special emphasis on his interaction with Booker T. Washington, his pioneering role in establishing the field of human ecology, and his recruitment and training of black sociologists. Then, beginning with the birth of academic sociology at the University of Chicago under Albion W. Small, the development of the sociological enterprise at Chicago is placed in its historical context. Finally, the central focus of the essay is a study of the career line, research, and theory of Frazier. Considerable attention will be given to the following topics: the ecological approach, black family studies, social stratification in the black community, the Frazier-Herskovits controversy over the

1. Daniel Patrick Moynihan, *The Negro Family: The Case for National Action* (Washington, D.C.: U.S. Government Printing Office, 1965).

intensity of African cultural survivals, Frazier's Brazilian fieldwork, and his critique of the concepts of his Chicago mentors.

A growing body of race-relations literature is being written from the perspective of the sociology of knowledge. In 1943 William T. Fontaine, a black professor of philosophy, asked whether there was any correlation between the black scholar's knowledge and the position of the black group in the American social order. In criticizing Fontaine's article, Frazier admitted "it would not be difficult to show that the research interests of many Negro scholars have been 'socially determined.'" Clearly Frazier believed that the contributions of black scholars in the social sciences could be studied profitably from the standpoint of the sociology of knowledge. His principal caution was that such study requires a more fundamental knowledge of the social position of various black scholars than most writers possess. This study focuses on the sociological contributions of Frazier, one of the "first generation" of professional black sociologists and perhaps Park's consummate student of race relations.[2]

This line of inquiry was suggested in a review of Myrdal's *An American Dilemma* by Ralph Ellison. Ellison encouraged a close analysis of the general relationship between American social science and "American Negro destiny" focusing on the following pairs of relationships: Robert E. Park and the Chicago School of Sociology; Booker T. Washington and Robert E. Park; Tuskegee Institute and the University of Chicago; American philanthropy and American social science. This approach recognizes that, compared with the natural and physical sciences, the internal status of sociology and the social sciences is only partial.

The development of sociology in the Old South is an extreme case that illustrates in bold relief the shaping influence on sociology of what Charles H. Page has called "native conditions" in the 1850s when the impending sectional crisis drove the South to desperate ends to generate a social philosophy supportive of sectional interests.[3] Some thinkers, like lawyers Henry Hughes of Mississippi and George Fitzhugh of Virginia, conceived the idea of applying the

2. William T. Fontaine, "Social Determination in the Writing of Negro Scholars," *American Journal of Sociology* 59 (1943), 303–13, with rejoinders by E. Franklin Frazier and Edward B. Reuter.

3. Charles H. Page, preface to *The Development of Modern Sociology*, by Roscoe C. Hinkle, Jr., and Gisella Hinkle (Garden City, N.Y.: Random House, 1954), v.

principles of the infant study of sociology to local southern situations. The result was the appearance of the earliest known works in English to carry the word *sociology* in their titles.[4] These works—*Treatise on Sociology, Theoretical and Practical* (1854) by Hughes and *Sociology of the South* (1854) by Fitzhugh—were almost exclusively concerned with the South's "Negro problem." Frazier called these works "the most extensive and important rationalizations of the [slave] system."[5] These reflections of native conditions in the development of social science in the United States are not isolated phenomena. Edward Shils accurately stated that social scientist's self-identification is more affected by particularistic attachments than is that of the natural scientists in the international intellectual community.[6]

Robert Ezra Park: Pioneer American Sociologist

Born in Harveyville (Lucerne County), Pennsylvania, on February 14, 1864, Park grew up and attended school in Red Wing, Minnesota. In 1887 he was awarded the Bachelor of Philosophy degree from the University of Michigan. He then embarked on a career as a reporter on daily newspapers in Minneapolis, Detroit, Denver, New York, and Chicago. In 1894 Park married Clara Cahill, daughter of a prominent Michigan attorney. After over a decade as a newspaperman, he returned to university life, studying in the departments of philosophy and psychology at Harvard University and receiving the Master of Arts degree in 1899. While at Harvard he studied psychology with Hugo Munsterberg and philosophy with Josiah Royce, William James, and George Santayana. After leaving Harvard, Park took his family to Berlin and Heidelberg, where he

4. H. G. Duncan and W. L. Duncan, "The Development of Sociology in the Old South," *American Journal of Sociology* 39 (Mar. 1933): 649–56; W. E. Dodd, "The Social Philosophy of the Old South," *American Journal of Sociology* 22 (1918): 735–46; and Richard M. Guess, "Henry Hughes, Sociologist, 1829–1862" (master's thesis, University of Mississippi, 1930).

5. E. Franklin Frazier, "Role of the Negro in Race Relations in the South," *Social Forces* 19 (Dec. 1940): 254.

6. Edward Shils, "Color, the Intellectual Community, and the Afro-Asian Intellectual," in *Color and Race*, ed. John Hope Franklin (Boston: Houghton Mifflin, 1966), 8.

studied with Georg Simmel (his only instructor in sociology) and Wilhelm Windelband. At Heidelberg, Park wrote a doctoral dissertation in German, "Masse und Publicum" ("The Crowd and the Public"), and was awarded the Doctorate of Philosophy in 1904.[7]

Upon returning to the United States, Park took a position as an assistant in philosophy at Harvard University but soon became interested in educational work among black folk. Shortly, under the auspices of the Massachusetts Commission for International Justice, he organized the American branch of the Congo Reform Association.[8] The Congo Reform Association was founded in March 1904 by E. D. Morel (George Edmond Pierre Achille Morel de Ville), a French-born British pamphleteer and reformer. Morel was, in the opinion of W. E. B. Du Bois, "no particular lover of Africans":

> In truth, his attitude toward the black man is that of the liberal Englishman: that is to say, he is opposed to the past atrocities and wants Africans helped in every benevolent and philanthropic way. He has, however, no conception of self-governing, independent black Africa. Indeed, he suspects and rather dislikes the educated African and certainly has no faith in his independent future. His attitude is best summed up in this word from his introduction. His book "seeks to lay down the fundamental principles of a humane and practical policy in the government of Africa by white men."[9]

Park admired Morel, giving this explanation of his feelings:

> I agree perfectly with what you say that this is not a fight against the Congo State alone, it is against slave labour in tropical Africa. It is

7. To my knowledge the only book-length biographical study of Park is Winifred Raushenbush, *Robert E. Park: Biography of a Sociologist* (Durham: Durham University Press, 1979). For an analysis of Park's early writings, see Stanford M. Lyman, *Militarism, Imperialism, and Racial Accommodation: An Analysis and Interpretation of the Early Writings of Robert E. Park* (Fayetteville: University of Arkansas Press, 1992).

8. There are conflicting reports concerning the sequence of events after Park returned to the United States. One account indicates that he became an assistant in philosophy at Harvard University but soon became interested in educational work among blacks, "Robert Ezra Park, 1864–1944," *Sociology and Social Research* 28 (1944): 308. See also Johnson, "Robert E. Park," 355. For background on the origins and activities of the Congo Reform Association, see Joseph O. Baylen, "Senator John Tyler Morgan, E. D. Morel, and the Congo Reform Association," *Alabama Review* 15 (1962): 117–32.

9. W. E. B. Du Bois, review of *The Black Man's Burden*, by E. D. Morel, *Nation* 11 (Sept. 25, 1920): 350–52.

simply the race issue in its most concrete form, that is, in the case where you have not merely the race but its appropriate environment, the soil on which it lives as an element in the problem. . . . There is nothing in the world that a man of your temperament or of my temperament would rather do in this world than fight just such iniquity as this in the Congo State. It is a great privilege to be allowed to do it. It is a luxury that few men can afford themselves. . . . To my way of thinking, politics, I mean politics of just the sort that you and I are engaged in, is the real business of human life.[10]

The black sociologist Charles S. Johnson perceived that Park accepted the Congo Reform Association position "not because of any strong interest in missions but because he was interested in the newspaperman's task of acquainting Americans with the brutal exploitation of African natives in the Belgian Congo."[11] According to Johnson, Park was preparing to travel to Africa to study the Congo situation firsthand when he met Booker T. Washington. Ernest Watson Burgess, Park's longtime colleague, office mate, and friend, indicates that Park went to Tuskegee "because he felt that the Negro problem was a significant one and that Booker T. Washington was dealing with it not sentimentally but realistically."[12]

Park described how he went to Tuskegee:

Another man, whom I knew longer and from whom I learned more than from any one of my other teachers, was Booker T. Washington. . . . I may as well tell how it happened. After six years of philosophy I was a little weary of the academic atmosphere. I wanted to renew my connections with the world of men and things. It happened that the foreign secretary of the Baptist Missionary Association,

10. Robert E. Park to E. D. Morel, Jan. 15, 1905, Morel Papers, British Library of Political and Economic Science at the London School of Economics. See A. Stengers and Jean Stengers's discussion of the Morel Papers in *Bulletin de la Commission Royale d'Histoire* 124 (1959).

11. Charles S. Johnson, "Robert E. Park: In Memoriam," *Sociology and Social Research* 28 (1944): 355. The records of the American Congo Reform Association apparently have been lost. Park wrote a series of exposes about the Congo situation, including "A King in Business: Leopold II of Belgium, Autocrat of the Congo and International Broker," *Everybody's Magazine* 15 (1906): 624–33 and "Terrible Story of the Congo," *Everybody's Magazine* 15 (1906): 763–72.

12. Ernest W. Burgess, "A Short History of Urban Research at the University of Chicago before 1946," revised version of a talk given before a seminar on "New Directions for Urban Research," reprinted as "Research and Urban Society: A Long View," in *Urban Sociology,* ed. Ernest W. Burgess and Donald J. Bogue (Chicago: University of Chicago, 1967), 3.

> Dr. Barbour, had just returned from abroad with some very gruesome evidence of the atrocities of King Leopold's rule in the Belgian Congo. He wanted some one to help him advertise conditions in that part of the world. As a result I became the first secretary of the Congo Reform Association. I was at that time very little of a missionary, and my experience as a newspaperman, had convinced me that reform was not enough. But the Congo looked to me like a "good story."
>
> In the course of the campaign to arouse public opinion on the subject of the Congo natives, I sought out everyone in the United States who knew anything about the so-called Congo Free State and anyone else who could be interested in the fate of the natives there. It was in this way that I met Booker Washington. . . . When, however, I told him [B.T.W.] that I was thinking of going to Africa; that there was, I had heard, at Lovedale, South Africa, an industrial school for natives, and that, if there was any solution for the Congo problem it would probably be some form of education, he invited me to come to Tuskegee. I went to Tuskegee to stay a few weeks, but I remained for seven years.[13]

Park worked closely with Washington throughout those seven years and in 1910 accompanied him on a tour of Europe. Upon their return from Europe, Washington and Park collaborated on an account of their findings published as *The Man Farthest Down: A Record of Observation and Study in Europe* (1912). At Tuskegee Park helped Washington develop educational programs based on the assumption that black folk would remain in the rural South.

Impressed with Park during a visit to Tuskegee, sociologist William I. Thomas invited him for a summer term at the University of Chicago in 1913. Park left Tuskegee and, with the urging of Thomas and department chairman Albion W. Small, stayed on at Chicago as professor of sociology until his retirement in 1929. During World War I, Park chaired the Joint Emergency Committee, and as head of the Chicago Urban League, he warned the public that the war had "disturbed the equilibrium of the races" and asked "what is going to happen when the Negro troops return from France?"[14] From 1929 to 1932 he traveled to the world's major racial frontiers, including India, Malaya, Brazil, and South Africa, and served as a guest

13. Robert E. Park, "Methods of Teaching: Impressions and a Verdict," *Social Forces* 20 (1941), 41.

14. Chicago Urban League, *Second Annual Report for the Fiscal Year Ended October 31, 1918*, cited in *From Race Riot to Sit-In* by Arthur I. Waskow (Garden City, N.J.: Doubleday, 1967), 40.

professor at the University of Hawaii and Peking's Yenching University. Then in 1936 Park emerged from retirement to serve as a visiting professor at Fisk University in a talent-studded social science division headed by one of his former students, Charles Spurgeon Johnson.[15] When he arrived at Fisk, Park had abandoned his earlier assumption, held while working under Booker T. Washington, that black folk would remain in the rural South and turned his attention to training blacks destined to move into urban areas.

Besides being generally acknowledged as the scholar most responsible for establishing collective behavior as a field of sociological study, Park was, by all accounts, a pioneer in the field of human ecology; his approach deeply influenced E. Franklin Frazier. Briefly, the subject matter of ecology is the interdependence between living things and their habitat. Human ecology is the study of humankind in relation to environmental conditions—climate, water, soil, natural resources, atmosphere—and to other plant and animal species, as well as its interaction with definable societies and cultures on Earth. The five basic areas of human ecology are population, social organization, position and function of power, migration, and changes in spatial distribution of populations through time. Plant and animal ecology began to develop as separate disciplines in the 1870s, but it was not until about 1920 that any significant work was done in human ecology. Park became interested in the implications of plant and animal ecology for the study of human communities, particularly the city. The approach developed by Park and his students came to be known by various names, including the "Chicago School of Human Ecology."[16]

Reacting against the highly abstract normative brand of sociology espoused by earlier sociologists, many of whom had ties with Protestant clergy, Park and Burgess warned their students that the study of society could not be both scientific and moralistic at the same time. According to Burgess, Park explicitly discouraged his

15. Werner J. Cahnman, "Robert E. Park at Fisk," *Journal of the History of the Behavioral Sciences* 14 (1978).

16. Ernest W. Burgess, "The Contributions of Robert Park to Sociology," *Sociology and Social Research* 29 (1945): 261. For further reviews of ecological work, see June Helm, "The Ecological Approach to Anthropology," *American Journal of Sociology* 67 (1962): 630–39; and Amos H. Hawley, "Ecology and Human Ecology," *Social Forces* 22 (1944): 398–405.

students' involvement in social protest: "Park told them flatly that the world was full of crusaders. Their role instead was to be that of the calm, detached scientist who investigates race relations with the same objectivity and detachment with which the zoologist dissects the potato bug."[17] Earle Fiske Young, who received a Ph.D. in sociology from Chicago in 1924, believed that Park had no interest in reform as such but regarded it merely as another social phenomenon requiring scientific analysis.[18] Ellsworth Faris, who was a graduate student at the University of Chicago and who later taught there, said that "Park was probably the only one who directly attacked the humanitarian attitude when it appeared among sociologists. More than once he drove students to anger or tears by growling such reproofs as 'you're another one of those damn do-gooders.' "[19]

While less conservative than Social Darwinist William Graham Sumner, Park and many of his pupils were bound by a similar fatalism. Park's observations of social conditions led him to acknowledge the power of what he liked to call "natural forces." His sociological system embodied a *systematic tendency* to ignore practically all possibilities of modifying the social effects of "natural forces" by conscious social intervention. He displayed a singular lack of interest for problems of *induced* social change. In sum, one of America's most prominent sociologists, who had a strong hand in the training of a cadre of black sociologists, held lukewarm views about the prospects of planned social change and social protest.

Park and the Sociological Enterprise at Chicago

After sketching the general outlines of Park's career, it is appropriate to describe briefly the activities centered around the Chicago School of Sociology and place them in their proper historical context.

17. Ernest W. Burgess, "Social Planning and Race Relations," in *Race Relations: Problems and Theory,* ed. J. Masuoka and Preston Valien (Chapel Hill: University of North Carolina Press, 1961), 17.

18. Earl Fiske Young, "A Sociological Explorer: Robert E. Park," *Sociology and Social Research* 28 (1944), 437.

19. Robert Ellsworth Faris, *Chicago Sociology, 1920–1932* (Chicago: University of Chicago Press, 1967), 35.

In 1890 the Hebraist William Rainey Harper became the first president of the new University of Chicago; this was to have a galvanizing effect on higher education. The university's far-reaching impact can be seen in microcosm in Chicago's role in the development of American sociology. Albion W. Small identified the central geographical location and the overall effect of the university on American education as key factors in Chicago's influence on the teaching of sociology.[20]

Among Chicago's social scientists were Charles R. Henderson, George E. Vincent, and William I. Thomas. During the 1893–1994 academic year, Thomas spent two quarters studying with Albion Small and Charles Henderson in the newly founded department of sociology. In 1894 Thomas began giving courses in sociology at Chicago and completed the doctorate in 1896. One element of President Harper's grand design, the university press, contributed in a bold way to Chicago's eminence in sociology. Late in the spring of 1895, after three years of effort, Harper decided to abandon an attempt to create a constituency for a university extension magazine. According to Albion Small, Harper one day abruptly remarked, "We have got to give up the *University Extension World.* It would be a pity for that subsidy to be transferred to anything but publication. Are you willing to be responsible for a journal of sociology?" Small took Harper's suggestion as a "dare," and, after brief consultation with Henderson, Thomas, and Vincent, reported that the group was ready to undertake such a publication. When the announcement was made that the *University Extension World* would become the *American Journal of Sociology,* the editors did not even have promises of enough material to fill an issue. Nevertheless, the first number was published in July 1895, and the journal went on to become one of the country's most respected journals of sociology.

The Chicago School of Sociology might be considered a movement of sociologists grouped around Robert E. Park that produced a large number of studies of urban society during the 1920s and had a large influence on urban sociology, community studies, and

20. For a brief biographical sketch of Small (1854–1926) and an evaluation of his writings and sociological thought, see John B. Edlefsen, "Albion Woodbury Small," *Sociology and Social Research* 39 (1955); 217–23.

the sociological analysis of occupations.[21] During this productive decade, according to Everett C. Hughes, who was there during that time, "a large number of men who entered sociology via the University of Chicago after a try at some other occupation fanned out over the country as members and chairmen of smaller colleges. It was not that Chicago had built up a monopoly; it was that the others had not shown much energy for initiative."[22]

Chicago sociologists viewed the city as a social laboratory to be studied in a broad interdisciplinary intellectual atmosphere. The involvement of the leading figures of the department of sociology with the other social sciences, evident even before World War I, became more pronounced in the 1920s as they maintained close contact with such figures as Charles Merriman, Harold D. Lasswell, Harold Gosnell, L. L. Thurstone, and Edward Sapir. According to Morris Janowitz, "the construction of the Social Sciences Research Building in 1929, as the first interdisciplinary center in the social sciences, served to house these men and the various departments. 'Eleven twenty-six,' as it came to be known (from its street address), made it possible for the small faculty and student body to be in continuous personal and intellectual contact: the term *social science* took on real meaning."[23]

Under Park's leadership, the Chicago School of Urban Sociology pioneered in the sociological study of ethnic and race relations, working through Hull House and other neighborhood centers. The analysis of interethnic mobility in terms of the "race relations cycle" of contact, conflict, accommodation, and assimilation characterized the work of the "school" during the 1920s and 1930s. The two outstanding theoretical bases of the Chicago studies were the application of the analogy derived from plant and animal ecology and the use of the theories of Tonnies and Durkheim that modern society evolved from communal relatively undifferentiated units into heterogeneous systems characterized by specialization and the division of labor. A regular program of research training in race relations,

21. See, for example, the retrospective view of Everett C. Hughes, "The Humble and the Proud: The Comparative Study of Occupations," *Sociological Quarterly* 11 (1970): 147–56.

22. Everett C. Hughes, review of *As a Tale That Is Told: The Autobiography of R. M. MacIver, American Journal of Sociology* 74 (1968): 193–94.

23. Morris Janowitz, foreword, *Chicago Sociology,* by Faris, ix.

continued until 1954, made the University of Chicago one of what Joseph S. Himes termed "the leading cases of empirical study of Negroes."

In Ernest W. Burgess's view, "the sociological studies of Chicago began with an article which Dr. Park wrote, 'The City: Suggestions for the Investigation of Human Behavior in the Urban Environment.' "[24] Park and Burgess taught the principles of sociology course while collaborating on *Introduction to the Science of Sociology* (1921), which is generally acknowledged as the first American textbook in sociology geared to research. In the late 1910s and early 1920s, Park taught courses on social survey, the newspaper, the Negro in America, the Negro in the Old South, and the crowd and the public. Horace Mann Bond, a black graduate student at Chicago during this period, was shocked when, one day in the seminar on Negro in the Old South, Park told his students: "The Negro is the lady of the races; delicately proportioned, small boned, devoted to the arts of music and dance, with exquisite manners, the utmost in politeness, she cannot bear to hurt anyone's feelings."[25]

Implicit in this statement, which irritated so many of the first generation of black sociologists, including E. Franklin Frazier, was Park's belief that different human populations were endowed with different *biologically transmitted* cultural capacities.

Edward Franklin Frazier and the Chicago School of Sociology

Some of the most prominent, productive, and influential black sociologists in the United States have been trained in the social and institutional setting of the Chicago "school" of sociology, and many of those trained before 1935 developed close personal relationships with Robert E. Park. Among them Frazier is considered by many to be perhaps Park's consummate student of race relations. Frazier was

24. Ernest W. Burgess, "Research and Urban Society: A Long View." Park's article appeared in the *American Journal of Sociology* 20 (1915): 577–612.

25. Horace Mann Bond, "Howe and Isaacs in the Bush: The Ram in the Thicket," statement distributed at the conference of the American Society of African Culture, New York, 1960, reprinted in *Apropos of Africa*, ed. Adelaide C. Hill and Martin L. Kilson (London: Frank Cass & Co., 1969). Morris Janowitz defended Park's use of the phrase "lady of the races" in a review of *Shadow and Act*, by Ralph Ellison, *American Journal of Sociology* 70 (1965), 733.

born to James Edward and Mary Clark Frazier in Baltimore, Maryland, on September 24, 1894. Horace R. Cayton, also a Park student and a black sociologist, once eloquently described Frazier's family background:

> Frazier overcame great odds to achieve his position of eminence as a social scientist. His father was a bank messenger who never had a day's schooling in his life. His paternal grandfather was a self-emancipated slave who bought his family's freedom. His mother was an ex-slave. At the family table young Frazier heard talk of slavery, of cruelty, of injustice—early he learned of the curious, contradictory ways of white folk. But the matrix of social and personal relations into which he was born—one calculated to humiliate, crush and rob the Negro of his manhood—failed to limit the horizon of the young man. Rather it put iron in Franklin's blood and steel in his backbone. He did not indulge in a self-hate which would have led to resignation and hopelessness. This social system which accorded no place which he could occupy with dignity, Frazier fought in fury and indignation. As a boy walking to school he would spit on the Johns Hopkins University building because he knew he could not aspire to enroll there.[26]

After graduating from Howard University with honors in 1916, Frazier taught at various schools in Alabama, Virginia, and Maryland. Frazier's critics who emphasize the pernicious influences of Park frequently overlook an obvious fact; Frazier was a mature, strong-willed, thirty-three-year-old adult when he began studying for the doctorate at the University of Chicago. Prior to that, as the Johns Hopkins University spitting episodes suggest, Frazier fought against racial bias in both individual and organized forms. When Frazier refused to pay a voting tax that was required in Alabama even though blacks were not allowed to vote, Tuskegee Institute paid it for him and took it out of his salary. In 1920, while studying at the New York School of Social Work, Frazier was jailed for picketing the film *The Birth of a Nation*.[27] Also during the 1920s Frazier wrote and published at his own expense a tract, "God and War," linking Christianity, capitalism, and international strife. "In common with most students of his generation," G. Franklin Edwards

26. Horace R. Cayton, "E. Franklin Frazier: A Tribute and Review," *Review of Religious Research* 5 (spring 1964): 137.

27. Arthur P. Davis, "E. Franklin Frazier: A Profile," *Journal of Negro Education* 31 (1962).

has remarked, "Franklin Frazier did not begin the study of sociology as an undergraduate."[28] Following those early teaching experiences Frazier had his first serious study of sociology at Clark University in Worcester, Massachusetts, during the 1919–1920 academic year and received the Master of Arts degree in 1920. His thesis topic, "New Currents of Thought among the Colored People of America," reflected his continuing interest in "the race problem." In 1920–1921 Frazier was a research fellow at the New York School of Social Work, and the following year he studied in Denmark on a fellowship from the American Scandinavian Foundation. On September 14, 1922, he married Marie Ellen Brown, the daughter of a distinguished black religious leader in North Carolina. Then, after a brief stay at Livingstone College in Salisbury, North Carolina, he accepted a position as instructor of sociology at Morehouse College and director of the Atlanta School of Social Work. While at Morehouse and before he began to study under Park, Burgess, and the other Chicago sociologists, Frazier began to display a recognizable environmental emphasis in seeking to explain the social conditions of black Americans. In a 1925 article in *Crisis* entitled "Eugenics and the Race Problem," he countered what he considered to be Albert Sidney Beckham's overly enthusiastic and uncritical acclaim for "eugenic control" as a solution to Negro problems.[29] In 1927, as the result of a hostile and emotional reaction by some elements of the white community of Atlanta to an article entitled "The Pathology of Race Prejudice," published in *Forum,* Frazier was forced to leave the city.[30] Ironically, Frazier was thereby presented with a chance to pursue the doctorate of sociology. He studied from 1927 to 1929 at the University of Chicago, serving as director of the research department of the Chicago Urban League during much of that time, and began teaching in the social sciences division at Fisk University in 1929. He was awarded the doctorate from Chicago in 1931, and his dissertation was published

28. G. Franklin Edwards, "The Contribution of E. Franklin Frazier to Sociology," *Journal of Social and Behavioral Sciences* 13 (1967), 25.

29. E. Franklin Frazier, "Eugenics and the Race Problem," *Crisis* 31 (Dec. 1925): 91–92.

30. In that article he had argued that in both race prejudice and mental disturbances the psychological mechanisms of dissociation and projection were operative and had made particular reference to the operation of projective mechanisms in white women who falsely accused black men of rape, suggesting that many accusations were products of wish fulfillment.

the following year by the University of Chicago Press under the title *The Negro Family in Chicago*. In 1934 Frazier became professor of sociology at Howard University and succeeded Kelly Miller as head of the department of sociology; he remained at Howard University until his death in 1962. In 1945 he became the first black president of the Eastern Sociological Society, and in 1948 he served as president of the American Sociological Association. During most of his career, Frazier lived and worked in the segregated city of Washington, D.C., in which relatively few restaurants served blacks and whites together. Frazier once described to the anthropologist Sidney W. Mintz "how he had to wear a woman's scarf and costume jewelry in order to eat—a self-appointed raja—with his white sociologist colleagues in a Washington, D.C. restaurant."[31]

For Frazier the term *race relations* encompassed the body of attitudes and sentiments of whites that establishes social distance between the races; the institutionalized practices that define the status of blacks; and the manner in which the black struggle for status in the social organization affects social distance between the races. He described how the relative isolation of the black population in American cities created a cultural community, paying particular attention to the spatial distribution of the black population, the history of black communities, and the black family. He found the spatial distribution of the black population to be particularly significant because it formed the basis of both group solidarity and class differentiation. Similarly, in his studies of black families, Frazier demonstrated that the expansion of the black community followed the growth of the city and that the process of expansion could be measured in rates of change in such items as poverty and home ownership. More specifically, in his doctoral study of black families in Chicago, Frazier was developing a technique for measuring different social and economic gradations from the standpoint of physical location. He employed an ecological analysis to show that the organization, disorganization, and reorganization of black family life in northern cities was closely tied to the economic and social structure of the black community, taking a definite *spatial pattern* which bore the imprint of the ecological organization of the larger community. In sum, as Frazier

31. Sidney W. Mintz, "Review Article: Slavery and the Slaves," *Caribbean Studies* 8 (1969): 65.

said, "the ecological organization of the community is the basis of social organization."[32]

Frazier's stance reflects the thinking of Ernest W. Burgess, with whom he worked closely in his studies of black family life. Burgess attempted to break down the tendency to treat residential segregation of white and black as unique isolated phenomenon of urban life. He presented a broader ecological framework in which residential segregation along racial lines was only one case in a larger process of urban segregation of racial and immigrant groups or economic and social classes.[33] Nathan Glazer has argued that, despite its genuine liberalism and progressivism, the entire Chicago School of sociologists shared the individualistic values of the times, which assumed that government played only limited roles in shaping economic and social life. From this perspective, social developments tended to be viewed as independent, almost natural movements, impervious to the political process. With the scholarly detachment so assiduously cultivated by Park and others there, the Chicago sociologist could study the transition of urban neighborhoods and hardly stop to consider whether this was desirable or undesirable, and whether political forces could modify such movements.[34]

Frazier was not uninterested in policies, but he emphasized that only through the understanding of the complicated processes of interaction among the various elements of society could we arrive at critical evaluation of policies and a realistic view of what is possible and what is desirable. In *The Negro Family in the United States,* for example, he carefully refrained from lecturing Americans about what they should do to realize their ideal of a democratic society but adhered strictly to the task of furnishing an authentic and richly documented account of the black experience in the United States.

Frazier's position on the possibility of "African survivals" in black American life was a major bone of contention during his career and remains controversial today in ongoing reformulations of the field of African American studies. Citing Robert Park's authority,

32. E. Franklin Frazier, "Desegregation as an Object of Sociological Study" (1961), reprinted in *Frazier on Race Relations,* 322.

33. Ernest W. Burgess, "Residential Segregation in American Cities," *Annals* 140 (1928): 105.

34. Nathan Glazer, foreword to *The Negro Family in the United States,* by E. Franklin Frazier, rev. ed. (Chicago: University of Chicago Press, 1966), xvi.

Frazier stated in 1931 that "our present knowledge of the conditions under which slavery was established in America leads us to believe that the Negro was completely stripped of his social heritage in the process."[35] Frazier engaged in a thirty-year running debate with the Africanist anthropologist Melville J. Herskovits, who claimed that African cultural survivals could be found in most areas of black American life. Meier and Rudwick reported that the debate between them had reached such intensity that one of their confrontations at the American Council of Learned Society's 1940 conference on Negro studies, "reportedly almost ended in a physical confrontation."[36] While this story may be apocryphal, it is clear that Frazier and Herskovits corresponded rather regularly, beginning as early as 1936, when Frazier invited Herskovits to give a paper at a three-day conference on the topic of "Imperialism in Africa" sponsored by the division of social sciences at Howard University.[37] Carter G. Woodson believed that it was while studying under Park at the University of Chicago that "Dr. Frazier was led erroneously to believe that the Negro transplanted from Africa to America retained very little of his African culture except his temperament."[38] Woodson also accused Frazier of being ashamed of his African heritage. Frazier's position on the Africanisms question and his knowledge of Africa and of African-derived populations in other parts of the Western hemisphere require careful consideration. During the 1940–1941 academic year, Frazier, funded through a fellowship from the John Simon Guggenheim Foundation, studied the Negro family in Bahia, Brazil, the most important center of what Melville and Frances Herskovits called "Afro-Brazilian customs."[39] During his study Frazier conducted interviews with Afro-Brazilian informants in Portuguese. One of his Bahian informants, an eighty-year-old man, told Frazier

35. E. Franklin Frazier, "The Changing Status of the Negro Family," *Social Forces* (1931): 386.

36. August Meier and Elliott M. Rudwick, *Black History and the Historical Profession* (Urbana: University of Illinois, 1986), 246.

37. E. Franklin Frazier to Melville J. Herskovits, Mar. 7, 1936, Herskovits to Frazier, Mar. 13, 1936, Frazier to Herskovits, Mar. 24, 1936, Herskovits to Frazier, Apr. 3, 1936, Melville J. Herskovits Papers, Northwestern University.

38. Carter G. Woodson, review of *The Negro in the United States*, by E. Franklin Frazier, *Journal of Negro History* 34 (July 1949).

39. Melville Herskovits and Frances Herskovits, "The Negroes of Brazil," *Yale Review* 32 (1943): 263.

how his father, a member of the Egba tribe, was brought to Brazil as a slave in the 1820s and freed in 1842. The father, following polygynous practices, had five wives. The informant had learned Yoruba from his parents, and being the child of his father's head wife, had accompanied his father to Africa and remained there eleven years perfecting his knowledge of Yoruba in an English mission school.[40]

Frazier's fieldwork in Brazil was part of his effort to discover the influence of African traditions and culture in the organization and functioning of Bahian families. This was a novel emphasis in that most previous investigations concerned with African survivals were interested primarily in religious practices and beliefs, music, dance, and folklore. Frazier's data supported, he thought, Arthure Ramos's assertion that slavery had drastically changed the social behavior of the African slaves and that African culture survived mainly in folklore. Whatever usage of African words and foodstuffs Frazier had found were transmitted, not through the family, but the *candomble*. In Frazier's words, "whatever has been preserved of African culture in the *candomble* has become a part of the folklore of the people."[41]

During the 1920s (and for quite some time thereafter), Frazier was struggling against notions that there was some kind of innate "racial" temperamental endowment of the Negro peoples that operated despite varying environmental conditions and radical cultural discontinuity. The 1920s was a decade during which pseudoscientific racism was at high tide. He was bent on demonstrating that "the racial experience of the Negro was unique because of historical and social forces rather than of biological inheritance" and seemed to fear that the African survivals position, perhaps unwittingly, left room for pseudoscientific racism to rush in through the back door.[42] Even Frazier, the most frequently cited authority taking the position that African cultural forces were completely or largely obliterated, was cautious enough to acknowledge that new information about African origins of the slaves would necessitate a reexamination of many assumptions, including the identity and extent of African

40. E. Franklin Frazier, "The Negro Family in Bahia, Brazil," *American Sociological Review* 7 (1942): 474–75.

41. Ibid., 478.

42. E. Franklin Frazier, "Racial Self-Expression," in *Black Protest Thought in the Twentieth Century*, ed. August Meier, Elliott Rudwick, and Francis L. Broderick, 2d ed. (Indianapolis: Bobbs-Merrill, 1971), 120.

survivals. In 1957 he wrote, "Only recently had we begun to secure sufficiently exact knowledge of the origin of the slaves brought to America to be in a position to identify African survivals."[43]

Over thirty years of increasingly intense and sensitive study of African historical cultures have elapsed since Frazier penned those lines. New and more precise information about the African origins of the American slaves has accumulated. The time for reexamination of assumptions has arrived. In the process many of Frazier's more radical catastrophist statements have been and will continue to be called into question, but it is important to understand that the vigor with which he dismissed what Stanley M. Elkins elsewhere has called "the African culture argument" derives from Frazier's adamant opposition to what he called "blood will tell sociology," which was regnant during the years of his intellectual formation.

Much of the evaluation of Park's impact on Frazier and of Frazier's impact on sociological studies of black Americans has been conducted by other Chicago-trained black sociologists. Among these is Abdul Ibn Alkalimat (Gerald McWorter) who once wrote:

> Robert Park was the most responsible in the social sciences for developing a liberal white game to run on black people. He and his colleagues at the University of Chicago were more responsible than any other graduate school for training black social scientists; perhaps their most important student was E. Franklin Frazier, a brother who was strong enough to collect a lot of important data, but who fell victim to theory based on the racist, white liberal ideology.[44]

Another Chicago-trained black sociologist, Oliver Cromwell Cox, was highly critical of Frazier's treatment of the black middle class in *Black Bourgeoisie* and speculated about what might have influenced Frazier's decision to write such a book.[45] The only factors Cox could identify were Frazier's schooling at Chicago, his approach to the study of race relations, and his peculiar strategy of self-promotion. Most pertinent of these for our discussion is what Cox termed "the

43. E. Franklin Frazier, *The Negro in the United States* rev. ed. (New York: Macmillan, 1957).

44. Gerald McWorter, "The Ideology of Black Social Science," *Black Scholar* 1 (1969): 28–35.

45. For a profile of Cox, see Herbert M. Hunter, "Oliver C. Cox: A Biographical Sketch of His Life and Work," *Phylon* 44 (1983).

Chicago outlook" derived from Frazier's training at the University of Chicago. Cox described the influence of Frazier's Chicago training as follows:

> It was Frazier's lot to be a student at the University of Chicago when three great sociologists, Ellsworth Faris, William F. Ogburn, and Robert E. Park, dominated the Department. I have become convinced from my personal association with and study of these men, that they were profound liberals in the sense in which that term is currently defined by direct action leaders. They were men possessed of praiseworthy attitudes towards Negroes, but still strongly opposed to any definition of them as fully equal to whites; they were willing to do many things *for* Negroes but sternly opposed Negroes taking such initiative as would move them along faster than a *proper pace;* and they would rather turn conservative than tolerate independent thinking or acting Negroes. One can discern most clearly the hand of Park on the intellectual life of Frazier. Park never fully sloughed off Darwinistic notions of cultural capacity among the races of man, and the vestige, apparently, was transmitted to Frazier.[46]

If, as Cox argued, Park never completely sloughed off Darwinistic notions about the cultural capacities of various racial groups and transmitted those notions to Frazier, I am convinced that Frazier soundly rejected these notions in his own work.

Swedish anthropologist Ulf Hannerz considers Frazier "the grand old man of the slavery school of interpretation" of black experiences.[47] In his interpretation of black family life Frazier suggested that the breakup of marriages since the beginning of slavery was an adaptation to a class-caste system. In viewing black family patterns as results of the adaptation to restricted social environments, however, Frazier did not deal adequately with the question of what the adaptations moved away from. The puritanical and cultural absolutist implication was that these patterns constitute an adaptation away from idealized mainstream American middle-class family norms. Again the trail of speculation as to why Frazier may have

46. Oliver C. Cox, introduction to *The Black Anglo-Saxons,* by Nathan Hare (New York: Collier Books, 1970), 28. For a brief assessment of Ogburn, see Carroll D. Clark, "The Contributions of William Fielding Ogburn," *Midwest Sociologist* 16, 2 (spring 1954): 3–6. Cox's critical assessment of the race relations theories of Park is included in Oliver C. Cox, "The Racial Theories of Robert E. Park and Ruth Benedict," *Journal of Negro Education* 13 (fall 1944): 452–63.

47. Ulf Hannerz, *Soulside: Inquiries into Ghetto Community and Culture* (New York: Columbia University Press, 1969), 73.

taken this tack leads to Chicago. Hannerz suggested that perhaps Frazier was "influenced in unfortunate ways by his contemporaries in the Chicago School of Sociology, as he saw mostly evils in the big city: anonymity, disorganization, lack of social supports and controls."[48]

Although these and other observers have criticized Frazier sharply for succumbing to the influence of Park and the Chicago School, it is clear that Frazier was not without criticisms of the theories of his Chicago mentors. It is true that Frazier once labeled Park an "objective student of social change rather than an advocate of a program," but in the same article he pointed out that Park and Burgess had drawn what he considered a false distinction between the position of a group or individual in the economic order and the status of an individual or group in the social order. Frazier wrote:

> The distinctions which these sociologists have made between the position of an individual or group in the economic order and the status of an individual or group in society tends to obscure the fact that the latter is dependent on the former; for in the final analysis the status of an individual or group is determined by his or its position in the economic organization. The rivalries, wars, and the subtler forms of conflict which determine the status of individuals and groups or the relations of superordination and subordination and social control in society are due fundamentally to the conflicting economic interests of the classes within the economic organization.[49]

Elsewhere and in a similar vein, Frazier said that Park's conception of the sociological approach to race relations may be criticized "on the ground that it fails to take into account the ecological, economic and political aspects of race relations, a conception which omits the dynamic aspects of race relations."[50]

The sociologist Bart Landry wrote in 1978 that "Frazier consistently followed the Marxian tradition in his own writings and analysis," and while this will undoubtedly continue to be debated, there

48. Ibid.

49. E. Franklin Frazier, "The Status of the Negro in the American Social Order," *Journal of Negro Education* 4 (1935): 293.

50. E. Franklin Frazier, "The Present Status of Knowledge Concerning Race Relations," in *Frazier on Race Relations*, 67.

is no doubt that Frazier both published in and served on the editorial advisory board of *Science and Society: A Marxian Quarterly.*[51]

Frazier underwent major surgery in December 1961. He resumed regular classroom duties, but then on May 17, 1962, Edward Franklin Frazier died at the age of 68. Nearly all of his writings dealt with race relations. Although in the United States a preoccupation with race relations has often meant a preoccupation with black Americans to the exclusion of all other groups, Frazier stressed that racial and cultural contacts must be viewed in a worldwide context. Earlier than most of his fellow social scientists, he realized the extremely limited value of race-relations research confined to interpersonal relations and attitudes. Frazier wrote,

> The analysis which I have given of the development of race relations in the Southern States is an illustration of the necessity to study social attitudes within the context of a system of social relations. But it is necessary to add a few remarks concerning the study of attitudes as the central problem of sociological analysis. For the social psychologist must take into a account the social context in which the attitudes are formed. Although this fact is generally recognized, there is still the tendency to treat attitudes without reference to their organic relation to the social situation. This is due largely to the attempt to introduce quantitative techniques and measurements and to take over uncritically the concepts of physical science.[52]

His work demonstrated that the truly sociological way to study race relations is in terms of *social structure.* In a memorial published in the *American Sociological Review,* his Howard University colleague G. Franklin Edwards noted that Du Bois had "once stated that Frazier stuck to his academic knitting."[53] In forty years of academic knitting Frazier fashioned a wide-ranging, richly detailed fabric depicting the institutional life and social organization of black Americans.

51. Bart Landry, "A Reinterpretation of the Writings of Frazier on the Black Middle Class," *Social Problems* (1978): 212 n. 4.

52. E. Franklin Frazier, "Theoretical Structure of Sociology and Sociological Research," *British Journal of Sociology* 4 (Dec. 1953), reprinted in *Frazier on Race Relations,* 7.

53. G. Franklin Edwards, "In Memoriam: Edward Franklin Frazier (1894–1962)," *American Sociological Review* 27 (1962), 891.

Part III

Reflections on the Black Middle Class and the Black Community

Between Scorn and Longing

Frazier's *Black Bourgeoisie*

ANTHONY M. PLATT

Introduction

E. Franklin Frazier is generally remembered for two legacies, both subjects of considerable controversy. First, his work on the African American family is praised by his supporters for its historical scope and empirical rigor but seen by his detractors as initiating the "pathological" critique of the matriarchal household and laying the groundwork for the notorious Moynihan report. Second, he is remembered, either fondly or irritably, as the scurrilous polemicist who cavalierly scribbled *Black Bourgeoisie* while enjoying gourmet lunches in Parisian bistros in the early 1950s.

When *Black Bourgeoisie* was finally published in the United States in 1957, two years after the French edition, Frazier became an instant celebrity, in demand as a speaker and a popular topic in the African American press. The American Sociological Association presented him with the MacIver Award, which he found amusing because he regarded the book as more of a debunking satire than serious scholarship. Nevertheless, he enjoyed the limelight during his last years and willingly made the rounds of sorority clubs, Negro associations, academic groups, and charity banquets, where he "flung critical and witty barbs at middle class colored Americans" in the audience. Undergraduates crowded into his classes at Howard to hear him berate them for aspiring to enter a world of delusions and "nothingness."[1]

1. For a typical account of a Frazier speech to a black sorority luncheon, see *Afro-American* (Aug. 26, 1958). "The black bourgeoisie suffers from 'nothingness' because when Negroes attain middle-class status, their lives generally lose both content and significance" (*Black Bourgeoisie*, 195).

And after his death in 1962, newly radicalized students discovered Frazier and used *Black Bourgeoisie* as ammunition against the old guard.

Frazier's work on the African American middle class is generally regarded as peripheral to his serious scholarship on race relations and the African American family. "Impressionistic" or "Menckenesque burlesque" are typical characterizations of *Black Bourgeoisie*.[2] The issues raised in Frazier's 1955 book, however, were both a political concern and object of serious study throughout his life, from his first polemic in 1918—in which he rebuked the "priestly class" for "turning nations into stone and the past into sacredness"—to his last essay in 1962—in which he berated black intellectuals for their "abject conformity in thinking." Even after his death, Frazier could still be heard expressing the same message, as disgruntled as ever with the "petty tyrants in the Negro churches" and "their counterparts in practically all other Negro organizations."[3] Frazier's own class history gave him particular insights into the dilemmas of the black bourgeoisie. His father, a bank messenger who died when his son was only ten years old, left Frazier with a fierce thirst for knowledge and upward mobility. While the young Frazier decided quite early that he was an atheist with an unshakable contempt for organized religion, he inherited his father's commitment to the Protestant ethic. At college, for example, he pursued a rigorous program of self-improvement. Coming from "a family that did not have a literary tradition," Frazier took four years of English courses in college, and "by writing a composition every day, I learned to write."[4] It was this kind of initiative and drive that allowed Frazier to climb out of the ghetto, yet it was not enough to enable him to succeed in the meritocratic world of the white professional middle classes. For all his accomplishments—he was the first African American president

2. G. Franklin Edwards, interviews by author, Washington, D.C., Nov. 23, 1970, and Mar. 30, 1989; Michael Winston, interview by author, Washington, D.C., Nov. 2, 1975; see also Edwards, *Frazier on Race Relations*, xviii.

3. Frazier, *God and War* (Unpublished pamphlet, c. 1918), 4; E. Franklin Frazier, "The Failure of the Negro Intellectual," *Negro Digest* (Feb. 1962): 31; E. Franklin Frazier, *The Negro Church in America* (New York: Schocken Books, 1966), 86. This book was first published in the United States in 1964.

4. E. Franklin Frazier, "The Role of the Social Scientist in the Negro College," in *The Civil War in Perspective: Papers Contributed to the Twenty-fourth Annual Conference of the Division of Social Sciences*, ed. Robert Martin (Washington, D.C.: Howard University Press, 1961), 11–12.

of the American Sociological Association (1948); author of *The Negro in the United States* (1949), the first serious textbook on the topic; consultant to the United Nations—he was never offered a tenure-track job in a predominantly white university, and the praise he received from his professional peers for his contributions as a *Negro* social scientist was intentionally backhanded.

Frazier certainly knew firsthand the world of the black bourgeoisie. As a young man he had learned a great deal about middle-class customs and foibles from his in-laws, pillars of religious respectability in North Carolina, and later he was sharply observant of his wife's social set in Washington, D.C. As somebody who taught in every kind of African American school and college, he was also well attuned to the nuances of segregated professionalism. He even once boasted that he wrote so truthfully about his subject matter because "I am a black bourgeois," but it is more likely that his powerful insights derived not so much from his membership in but rather from his marginality to a stratum that served as both a refuge and a prison.[5]

Like the "scholarship boys" in the English working class of the 1950s, captured so poignantly by Richard Hoggart, Frazier wavered between "scorn and longing." On the one hand, he was "equipped for hurdle-jumping" and had "been trained like a circus-horse, for scholarship winning." On the other hand, he was "at the friction-point of two cultures," uprooted from a sense of moorings, "gnawed by self-doubt," still the odd man out whose ability was both "a mark of pride and almost a brand."[6]

Frazier's lifetime work on the middle class was complex and contradictory, never fixed or simpleminded. By the time he wrote *Black Bourgeoisie,* late in his life and at a time of growing cynicism and despair, his views had gone through various permutations and transformations.

A Social Conception of Wealth

In the 1920s Frazier's perspective on the black bourgeoisie was extraordinarily eclectic, a mixture of ideas that he had gleaned from

5. Quoted by Davis, "Frazier: A Profile," 435.

6. Richard Hoggart, *The Uses of Literacy* (1957, reprint, London: Penguin Books, 1984), 291–304.

W. E. B. Du Bois, Booker T. Washington, and the social democratic socialism of the *Messenger* crowd. From Du Bois, Frazier borrowed the principle that the "Talented Tenth" had a moral and social responsibility to provide cultural, political and economic leadership in African American communities. While an undergraduate at Howard (1912–1916), Frazier heard Du Bois lecture about contemporary issues, and he listened carefully when the leader of the New Negro movement appealed to students' idealism, urging them to pursue careers that would give them the joy of accomplishment and social responsibility rather than the "rolling up of wealth."[7]

After he left Howard, Frazier was impressed with such organizations as the Neighborhood Union in Atlanta and the Fort Valley High and Industrial School in Georgia, where teachers, social workers, and ministers worked hard to build indigenous community institutions.[8] In this sense at least he shared Booker T. Washington's prescription for self-reliance. In 1921–1922 Frazier traveled to Denmark to study the farm cooperatives and rural schools, which, a decade earlier, had demonstrated to Washington "that it pays to educate the man farthest down." Frazier was similarly impressed with the cooperative movement in Denmark and thought that southern blacks could learn from an economic system that combined the best of individual thrift and collective methods of production and distribution. Frazier was an avid reader of the *Messenger,* which at that time was urging the beleaguered black petty bourgeoisie to embrace a cooperative system of economics.[9]

When Frazier went to teach social work in Atlanta in 1922, he was hopeful that credit unions, cooperative marketing, and other forms of collective enterprise would develop in the South. "A great step towards economic emancipation," he wrote in his first article for *Crisis,* "could be achieved through the development of cooperative enterprises in many centers of Negro population." Such a program, he

7. *Howard University Journal* (Apr. 17, 1914): 2–3.

8. See, for example, E. Franklin Frazier, "Neighborhood Union in Atlanta," *Southern Workman* (Sept. 1923): 437–42; "A Community School," *Southern Workman* (Oct. 1925): 459–64.

9. Booker T. Washington, *The Man Farthest Down: A Record of Observation and Study in Europe* (New York: Doubleday, Page, 1912), 340; E. Franklin Frazier, "The Cooperative Movement in Denmark," *Southern Workman* (Oct. 1923): 479–84; see also, A. Philip Randolph, "The Crisis in Negro Business," *Messenger* (Mar. 1922): 220–21.

argued, offered "safe investment opportunities for small quantities of capital" and was "in harmony with the present tendency towards the democratization of wealth. It is needless for us to go through the cruder stages of individualistic enterprise before we reach a social conception of the nature of wealth." Frazier hoped that black businesses would strive toward "true industrial democracy" and facilitate a "wide distribution of the economic surplus of the group."[10]

Frazier's brief experience with cooperatives in Denmark guided his political and economic views for several years. In 1925 he was still trying to convince an old friend that cooperatives were the "best means " to "amass capital through the mobilization of small amounts."[11] By 1928, however, he recognized that with the failure of "black radicals" to go south and teach "landless peasants any type of self-help," the cooperative movement was now a utopian vision, promising nothing but false hopes. A few years later when Du Bois flirted with a cooperative program, Frazier now dismissed the idea for its romanticism and economic stupidity. "What could be more fantastic," he asked in 1935, than Du Bois's "program for a separate non-profit economy within American capitalism?"[12] This disenchantment with the possibility of democratically controlled economic enterprises led Frazier to a much more realistic and pessimistic assessment of African American entrepreneurs.

La Bourgeoisie Noire

Frazier's critique of the black bourgeoisie was alluded to in various articles during the 1920s, hinted at in his essay for Alain Locke's *The New Negro,* and fully elaborated for the first time in 1928 in an article written for *Modern Quarterly.* As with his initial optimism about cooperatives, so Frazier hoped that black entrepreneurs would do

10. E. Franklin Frazier, "Cooperation and the Negro," *Crisis* (Mar. 1923): 228–29; E. Franklin Frazier, "Some Aspects of Negro Business," *Opportunity* (Oct. 1924): 293–97; E. Franklin Frazier, "Cooperatives: The Next Step in the Negro's Business Development," *Southern Workman* (Nov. 1924): 508.

11. Frazier to "Dock" Steward, Jan. 3, 1925, E. Franklin Frazier Papers, Moorland-Spingarn Research Center, Howard University.

12. See, for example, E. Franklin Frazier, "La Bourgeoisie Noire," *Modern Quarterly* (Nov. 1928): 82–83; E. Franklin Frazier, "The Du Bois Program in the Present Crisis," *Race* (winter 1935–1936): 13.

their part to raise "the general economic level of our group" rather than aspire to "peaks of affluence to dazzle the mob." On the basis of his apparent enthusiasm for the potentiality of African American business, Alain Locke sought him out to contribute an essay to *The New Negro* about the "real Negro economic start" that was under way in Durham, North Carolina.[13]

In the famous Durham article Frazier attempts to straddle the fence. At first reading, it is a purely descriptive and appreciative discussion of how the "Negro is at last developing a middle class" and acquiring the "spirit of modern enterprise" in banking and insurance. A close reading, however, reveals nuances of irony and parody submerged within its uncritical ambience. The black bourgeoisie, noted Frazier, has "the same outlook on life as the middle class everywhere. . . . White men have recognized these men as the supporters of property rights. They know these men would no more vote for Debs than they. Yet, there are still Jim Crow cars in North Carolina, and the Negro is denied civil and political rights." These subversive subtexts, however, constituted a fraction of the overall article, which, like the total contents of *The New Negro,* were designed, in Locke's words, to "celebrate the attainment of a significant and satisfying new phase of group development, and with it a spiritual Coming of Age."[14] Perhaps Frazier decided to be diplomatic for once; perhaps he settled for a bland neutrality because it was flattering to be included in Locke's coterie. Whatever Frazier's motivation, the Durham article, though not explicitly misrepresenting his views, did not accurately represent them.

In the late 1920s, Frazier tried to sort out his ambivalence about the cultural renaissance in African American urban centers. On the one hand, he participated in and was recognized as a leader of the New Negro movement. On the other, he regarded its development with skepticism and mistrust. Even when he was at his most optimistic about the progressive and social role that black-owned businesses could play in local communities, he always had his doubts and was on the lookout for betrayal. In the early 1920s, for example, Frazier endorsed the *Messenger*'s views about the need for

13. Frazier, "Aspects of Negro Business," 293–97; Locke to Frazier, c. 1925, Frazier Papers.

14. E. Franklin Frazier, "Durham: Capital of the Black Middle Class," in *The New Negro,* ed. Alain Locke, 333–40, 16.

self-defense and meeting white violence with black violence—what he described as a "positive moral force"—and was very critical of "those Negro leaders who through cowardice and for favors deny that the Negro desires the same treatment as other men." He hated "this sort of self-abasement" posturing as "Christian humility." To make his point, he recalled the example of a white philanthropist who donated large sums of money for black education in the South. All went well until she attended a meeting where she met " 'Negroes as cultured and as intelligent as white people.' " She left, "guilty and dismayed," determined to never support this cause again. "Her attitude towards Negroes," concluded Frazier, "was primarily that of a kindly lady who has sponsored a society for the prevention of cruelty to animals, but naturally resents rescued dogs, for example, assuming roles reserved for homo sapiens."[15]

Looking for an opportunity to correct the favorable impressions of the New Negro that might have been communicated by his Durham article, Frazier seized his chance when V. F. Calverton, editor of the leftist *Modern Quarterly,* asked him to submit "an article on the harmful influence of bourgeois psychology on the Negro movement, or something of the sort."[16] Some two weeks later, Frazier completed his critique of "La Bourgeoisie Noire," titled in French, suggests Harold Cruse, "no doubt to camouflage his Negro self-criticism."[17] Frazier may have shown some prudence in his choice of title, but the contents were quite candid. Gone was the oblique innuendo of the Durham piece.

There are essentially two themes in "La Bourgeoisie Noire." First, Frazier attempted to explain why "the Negro, the man farthest down in the economic as well as social scale, steadily refuses to ally himself with radical groups in America." To do this, he contested the widely held notion that the African American community was monolithic and homogeneous, pointing out that it was "highly differentiated" and those industrial workers, who were more likely to have a revolutionary consciousness, constituted only a small percentage of black

15. E. Franklin Frazier, "The Negro and Non-Resistance," *Crisis* (Mar. 1924): 213–14; Frazier quoted in "Opinion of W. E. B. Du Bois," *Crisis* (June 1924): 58–59; E. Franklin Frazier, "A Note on Negro Education," *Opportunity* (Mar. 1924): 76.

16. Eileen Hood to Frazier, Feb. 29, 1928, Frazier Papers.

17. Cruse, *Crisis of the Negro Intellectual,* 154.

workers. Second—and here Frazier propels himself into lifelong controversy—he analyzed the conservative role played by the new, rising middle class and its cultural spokesperson, the New Negro, in ensuring that "bourgeois ideals are implanted in the Negro's mind." He sadly noted the demise of the postwar black radical movement, typified by the *Messenger* which had degenerated from an "organ of the struggling masses" to a "mouthpiece of Negro capitalists." Frazier was critical of the New Negro movement, not because of its nationalism, but because under the encouragement of its white patrons, it had retreated into a narrow and depoliticized concept of culture. Black cultural workers were willing to settle for "Negro in Art Week" in return for agreeing "not to compete with the white man either politically or economically." The New Negro movement, concluded Frazier, "looks askance at the new rising class of black capitalism while it basks in the sun of white capitalism." Meanwhile, black businessmen were by now only interested in conspicuous consumption; a "society of equals" was the last thing on their minds.[18]

In the same way that Frazier brought a class analysis to bear on cultural issues, so he also refused to accept a view of African American communities as uniform, passive victims of white racism. What made Frazier's approach controversial and subversive was his exploration of the dynamics of collusion and collaboration, notably the opportunism of "Negro leaders who through cowardice and for favors deny that the Negro desires the same treatment as other men."[19] This was hardly a popular endeavor given the prevailing efforts of organizations like the NAACP and NUL to focus on how all blacks were equally oppressed by racism. To Frazier, many African American leaders were the descendants of the "waiting men" who had betrayed Denmark Vesey. From early on in the 1920s he had little faith in the new urban middle class, who, on the basis of "a little education or turn of fortune," all too readily turned its back on the "mass of Negroes" and was eager to "damn the black, greasy, boisterous Negro peasant in one breath and boast of their pride in Negro ancestry in the next." Similarly, he had little patience for interracial ambassadors, well-meaning black and white liberals who encouraged cooperation without challenging the roots of segregation. To

18. Frazier, "La Bourgeoisie Noire."
19. Frazier quoted in "Opinion of W. E. B. Du Bois," 59.

the New Negro crowd, in the words of historian David Lewis, "there was nothing wrong with American society that interracial elitism could not cure." Frazier, however, had nothing but contempt for any program that hinted of paternalism or noblesse oblige. "The Negro does not want love. He wants justice."[20]

Not surprisingly, Frazier's critique of academic do-gooders and civil rights careerists did not endear him to most of his professional colleagues. Accordingly, he received considerable criticism from some quarters. For example, as Oliver Cox correctly pointed out, Frazier's class analysis was theoretically imprecise and stretched almost beyond recognition Marxist conceptions of productive and economic relations. Frazier's muddled middle class included skilled workers and foremen, service and clerical workers, and professionals and petty entrepreneurs. Frazier took this kind of criticism seriously. "The term 'middle class' as used here," he wrote in his 1949 textbook, "refers to the class having an intermediate status between the upper and lower classes in the Negro community. Only a relatively small upper layer of this class is 'middle class' in the general American meaning of the term." Even though Frazier's framework focused on political and cultural factors, his overall analysis suffered from a lack of economic sophistication. The black bourgeoisie was, of course, in reality a petit bourgeoisie, but Frazier's writings told us very little about the relations of this stratum to the grand bourgeoisie or the corporate economy. This was a weakness that Frazier himself recognized and tried to correct in his last major work, *Race and Culture Contacts in the Modern World* (1957).[21]

Embittered Critique

Frazier's assessment of the black bourgeoisie in 1928 formed the basis of his later writings on this topic; his views hardly changed in thirty years. He elaborated his critique, deepened his analysis, and

20. Frazier, *Negro in the United States* (1949), 91; E. Franklin Frazier, "The Negro's Struggle to Find His Soul" (Unpublished essay, c. 1928), 7–8; David L. Lewis, *When Harlem Was in Vogue* (New York: Oxford University Press, 1989), 115; Frazier, "The Negro and Non-Resistance," 213.

21. Cox, introduction to *Black Anglo-Saxons*, 15–31; Frazier, *Negro in the United States* (1949), 301.

became more vitriolic in the 1950s, but at the core was the argument he had formulated in the 1920s. Through the 1930s, he sustained his fierce attack on African American leadership, accusing Du Bois of aspiring to be "king" of the "Black Ghetto" and exposing in James Weldon Johnson and other civil rights leaders opportunism and an unwillingness to "risk their own security." As for black businessmen, they dreamed of a "Black Utopia where the black middle class could exploit the black workers without white competition."[22]

After World War II, Frazier found his critique confirmed by the growth of an urban petty bourgeoisie, as lawyers, realtors, and shop owners took their places alongside the teachers and preachers who had traditionally wielded local power within black communities. This stratum, argued Frazier, had quickly developed "vested interests" in the "system of segregation," from which they derived the "exclusive enjoyment of . . . social and material rewards." His 1949 textbook, bolstered by Abram Harris's *The Negro as Capitalist* and other recent studies, reiterated his critique of the "marginal position of Negro enterprises" and "their insignificant role in the economy of the nation."[23]

In the last years of his life, Frazier returned to the issues that had preoccupied him during the 1920s. The publication of *Black Bourgeoisie* plus the resurgence of the civil rights movement in the South reawakened his interest. The book contained nothing new in the way of analysis or interpretation, though its style was even more acerbic and polemical than before. Here was the familiar history of stratification within black communities, the expose of the "myth of Negro business"—sustained, noted Frazier with a new turn of phrase, by "Negro businessmen [who] can best be described as 'lumpen-bourgeoisie' "—and a savage demystification of the "world of make-believe into which the black bourgeoisie has sought an escape from its inferiority and frustrations in American society."[24]

The next notable shift in Frazier's analysis of the black bourgeoisie occurred when he came into contact with Third World intellectuals

22. Frazier, "Du Bois Program," 11–13; "Quo Vadis?" *Journal of Negro Education* (Jan. 1935): 129–31; E. Franklin Frazier, "Some Effects of the Depression on the Negro in Northern Cities," *Science and Society* (fall 1938): 497.

23. E. Franklin Frazier, "Human, All Too Human: The Negro's Vested Interest in Segregation," *Survey Graphic* (Jan. 1947): 74–75, 99–100; Frazier, *Negro in the United States* (1949), 409, 412.

24. Frazier, *Black Bourgeoisie*, 145, 195.

and leftists during his two years (1951–1953) in Paris as chief of the Division of Applied Social Sciences at UNESCO. As a result of this exposure to global issues, he began to compare the African American middle class with "colored middlemen" and "compradors" around the world. He was struck by the similarities between the black bourgeoisies back home, "increasingly bewildered and frustrated in the white man's world," and the new native bourgeoisie of decolonized nations, who, in the words of one commentator, were "like derelicts, frantically seeking some foothold of security for body and mind." Frazier relearned the important lesson that it was not inevitable that the middle classes play a conservative and co-opted role. A choice had to be made, sides had to be taken. Frazier pointed to the positive example of Kwame Nkrumah, future president of Ghana, who expressed "a deep understanding and sympathy for the aspirations of the masses of Africans [and] wanted to make the nationalistic movement a mass movement."[25]

Increasingly, Frazier was impressed by nationalism in Africa and much more hopeful about its revolutionary potential than about the potential of its counterpart in the United States. Though he was encouraged by the civil rights movement stirring in the South and welcomed the new "militant spirit" of college students, he continued to argue that African American leadership "has no sense of responsibility to the Negro masses and exploits them whenever an opportunity offers itself." He warned the new African nations to look out for "American Negroes [who] may go to Africa as advisers and specialists" because "they will go as Americans representing American interests, not African interests." When asked in 1959 by *Presence Africaine* "What can the American Negro contribute to the social development of Africa?" his embittered response was, "Very little." A few weeks before his death in 1962, Frazier's last essay was published in *Negro Digest.* In "The Failure of the Negro Intellectual" he sounded a familiar theme, condemning his colleagues for failing "to dig down into the experience of the Negro and provide the soul of a people." Do not "run from Du Bois and Paul Robeson," he pleaded.[26] Despite his political differences with Du Bois

25. E. Franklin Frazier, *Race and Culture Contacts in the Modern World* (New York: Alfred A. Knopf, 1957), 293, 295, 300.

26. E. Franklin Frazier, "The New Negro," *Nation* (July 7, 1956): 7–8; E. Franklin Frazier, "The New Negro Middle Class," in *The Negro Thirty Years Afterward*

and Robeson over the years—whether it was Du Bois's call to "close ranks" during World War I or Robeson's uncritical defense of the Communist Party—they were heroic figures to Frazier because they risked their own personal security, willingly stood up to all kinds of establishments, and held their ground, no matter how unpopular their views. Ideology aside, Frazier admired this kind of intransigence of principle and personal stubbornness. Even after Du Bois was hounded in the witch-hunts of the 1950s and abandoned by most liberals, black and white, Frazier refused to stop his public support of the "man who raised the big moral questions having to do with racism, exploitation, and imperialism."[27]

In Frazier's last decade he became quite despondent about the prospects for equality in the United States. His previous polemics and social criticism had generally included proposals or counterproposals. Now they became one-sided, mostly critiques with little program, and there was a predominant edge of cynicism to the "enfant terrible," as he had once liked to call himself. From his undergraduate days at Howard through the 1930s, Frazier had sustained his commitment, shaped by social movements and innovative radical politics that attempted to unite struggles for economic and social justice. Though he always operated on the fringe of organizations and protected his ideological independence, he was deeply involved in the political culture of the civil rights, socialist, and nationalist movements. As these movements collapsed after World War II and he searched for a new identification in the context of global movements, Frazier's political commitments within the United States became sporadic and more vicarious, and Frazier became increasingly disillusioned with the possibility that such commitments by themselves could be effective. During the 1950s he had become alienated from both a defensive Left and an increasingly anticommunist and legalistic NAACP. He and many of the people he admired, espe-

---

(Washington, D.C.: Howard University Press, 1955), 26–32; E. Franklin Frazier, "What Can the American Negro Contribute to the Social Development of Africa?" in *Africa, Seen by American Negroes,* ed. John Davis (Paris: Presence Africaine, 1959), 263–78; Frazier, "Failure of the Negro Intellectual," 34, 36.

27. Marie Brown Frazier, interview by author, Washington, D.C., Nov. 2, 1975. Du Bois left the country in disgust and lived the last years of his life in Ghana. Frazier, out of respect for Du Bois and support for Kwame Nkrumah, bequeathed his library to the University of Ghana.

cially Robeson and Du Bois, were ostracized by the overwhelming majority of the black bourgeoisie, who succumbed to the pressures of McCarthyism. The "waiting men" had returned to close the circle of betrayal.

Unfortunately, his subjectivity got the better of him in his last years as he became more and more estranged from political movements in the United States. His critiques of the black bourgeoisie sounded increasingly dogmatic because he continued to apply an analysis that did not take into account changing conditions in the 1950s. For example, his last book, *The Negro Church in America,* published posthumously in this country, stressed the "stifling domination" that religious leaders exercised over African American communities. It was an old and plausible argument that he had made for several years, quite consistent with his overall assessment of the middle class. But in the mid-1950s, when he was writing this book, sectors of the Negro church had begun to play a prominent and militant role in the civil rights movement. His failure to address these contradictions and possibilities—as he did when he examined political movements in Africa and Asia in *Race and Culture Contacts in the Modern World*—made Frazier's analysis rigid and revealed how out of touch he was with the new activism.

Conclusion

A historical journey through Frazier's writings on the black bourgeoisie suggests a much more complex and contradictory analysis than that commonly associated with the fiery and disillusioned dogmatist of the late 1950s. Overall we have much to appreciate and reconsider in his work. At a time when African Americans were being reduced to homogeneous stereotypes—"saints" or "stones," to use his phrase—he fought to document the diversity and complexity of black families, communities and politics. However economically ingenuous, he recognized the importance of class analysis and the political contradictions raised by middle-class leadership of mass movements. He continually urged his peers who, like himself, had been both smart enough and lucky enough to climb out of misery always to remember their cultural roots and their social obligations. Do not be "seduced by dreams of final assimilation," he told them.[28] With African American businesses as marginal to the corporate economy as they were thirty years ago, with the black middle class still on the periphery of national political power, and with the New Right recruiting its first significant cadre of black neoconservatives, Frazier's insights seem as fresh and heretical as ever.

28. Frazier, "Failure of the Negro Intellectual," 26–36.

Frazier's *Black Bourgeoisie*

Talented Tenth or a Parasitic Class?

JOHN H. BRACEY

This essay will draw heavily on my own experiences growing up in Washington, D.C., in the 1940s and 1950s, my subsequent study of the writings of African American sociologists, and my personal experience with E. Franklin Frazier at Howard University.

Howard University in the 1950s

I had the privilege of knowing E. Franklin Frazier. I grew up on Howard's campus. My mother taught at Howard in the school of education. She also had been a student at the University of Chicago in the late 1920s and early 1930s when Frazier, Lorenzo Turner, Bertram Doyle, and that remarkable group of black scholars were there. I myself attended Howard University for one year. My memories of Frazier consist of walking up the hill from Lucretia Mott Elementary School, which was on Fourth Street (the original building has been replaced with a parking lot), crossing the main quadrangle on Howard's campus, going to Frederick Douglass Hall, sitting in a corner of my mother's office, and listening to fascinating arguments between people like Frazier and John Hope Franklin, Sterling Brown, and Emmett Dorsey.

I almost always took Frazier's side, because Frazier always seemed to get in the last word or the best word or the most interesting word. He also was one of the people who noticed that I was in the room and often would turn to me and say "young doctor, what do you think about all of this?" Despite President Mordecai Johnson's attempts to stifle Frazier, he was regarded as a major intellectual force at Howard and a major influence on serious students. I recall two incidents by way of illustration. One took place at a freshman assembly at Howard during the fall of 1959. Freshman assembly was a required weekly activity. You had a numbered seat, graduate assistants took the roll, and you were subjected to "longwinded" talks about "uplift," "lifting and climbing," and being a "credit to your race." At the first one I attended—there were three speakers. First was the head of the business school, who talked about the need to go into business and to lift up the race by getting involved in the world of business and making a lot of money. Next was the head of the philosophy department. I'm hard-pressed to this day to figure out what he said. Third was Frazier. Frazier walked up to the microphone and said look, the first guy talked about making a lot of money. There are plenty of white folks who don't have a lot of money; why did we think we're going to do better than them? He then said, my philosopher friend is a very learned man, but he wasn't talking about anything we could understand. Frazier concluded his brief remarks by saying, "My name is Ed Frazier. I teach sociology. Come talk to me in my office if you want to find out what's going on around here." And we just hollered, laughed, jumped up, and stamped our feet and had to be called back to order. That was who Frazier was to us.

This all took place at the end of the McCarthy era. There still was a tremendous amount of fear and repression. (I remember my mother getting a visit from the FBI because she was a member of the Book Find Club, which had been labeled communist-influenced.) Yet, Frazier brought to campus C. Wright Mills, the most famous radical sociologist of his day. He was not welcome at many white campuses, but he certainly spoke at Howard. I went to hear him. Anticolonial leaders such as Tom Mboya of Kenya also came to speak at Howard because of Frazier's initiatives. The textbook for the introduction to sociology course was *Work, Culture and Society.* The chapter on work included selections from the writings of Karl Marx, which we were being told everywhere else were not to be read. We didn't know what to do. We freshmen were assigned to read a section of *Das Kapital* on work and alienated labor, surplus value, and so on. We sat down, young, middle-class, black people and diligently went through our Karl Marx. I don't think Senator McCarthy ever knew or cared enough to come to a black school to find out what we were doing. There also was the incident when Frazier was invited to go to France to work with UNESCO. When he went down to get his passport, State Department officials informed him that he could not receive a passport because he was a radical and had communist tendencies, and, therefore, his travel was not in the national interest. Frazier said that's fine, I didn't ask to go to France. The United Nations asked me to go to France. He said, I have plenty of work to do. I'm going home. Frazier just walked out, got a cab, and came back to Howard. By the time he got back to Howard someone in the State Department had called somebody else, who called Frazier to say will you please come down and get your passport. He said no. I already took one trip, I'm not taking anymore trips downtown today. If you want me to have a passport you bring it to me. And some white junior bureaucrat got a cab from the State Department, came to Howard's campus, and brought E. Franklin Frazier his passport. That's the kind of person Frazier was. And that's the context within which, as I grew up, I understood Frazier to be working. Frazier's ideas did have importance. He also used to jig me about writing a biography of him when I was getting a little older. He would say, what are you going to do when you go to college? And I would answer, I don't know. I'll pick some useless major. Then he would say, well, I'm as useless as anybody, why don't you write about me? I never quite took that seriously, but I still have my autographed copies of his books, and I read virtually everything he wrote. I've come to the conclusion that Frazier, who never left for a white school, stayed at Howard for the same reasons that Sterling Brown and the others stayed, for the same reasons that scholars like Benjamin Quarles stayed at Morgan State. They were committed to the project of educating black people. And they complained from time to time that the students could be more serious and better prepared and that they themselves could have lighter teaching loads. I think they had a deep commitment to the people of whom they were a part. And I think Frazier's criticisms are directed most harshly at black people not because he hated himself, or didn't like being black, but because he thought that African Americans as a people should be doing much, much more than they were doing.

One last preliminary thought, Frazier deeply, deeply hated the time wasted by the Washington middle class: the canasta and whist parties, the time spent shopping and buying shoes, and so forth created a lot of the examples in *Black Bourgeoisie.* The anger emerged in the days when Frazier would come home from work to face a world he just couldn't take anymore. The amount of time and energy spent on play really did bother Frazier. And that ambience also had penetrated Howard, where the only time you stood in line without complaining was to get a table at the card room, and you wanted a good table by a window so you could watch the ebb and flow of the other students to and from classes.

On the other hand, it was the same middle class, the exact same middle class, that set up the law school at Howard and that produced that cadre of constitutional lawyers who were attacking the legal foundations of Jim Crow. It's the exact same middle class, same people. The exact same people you're swimming with at Highland Beach or whose children you were going to parties with were the same people who were driving relentlessly through the legal system on the way to the Supreme Court to win desegregation cases. And when the sit-in demonstrations started, it was the children of the same middle class that Frazier was attacking that led the demonstrations on the eastern shore of Maryland or in downtown Washington, D.C. I was one of them. And what I learned most from Frazier was to not be like the people in *Black Bourgeoisie.* If that's what we were doing with our lives, we should stop and think about it. And there was an impulse that came out of *Black Bourgeoisie* that made a whole generation of young people in the black middle class say that whatever we want to be, we don't want to be that. And I think that's what Frazier's point was. He held up this mirror and said, look at the waste, look at the foolishness you can get involved in. Do you really want to do that? And at Howard University during this time Karon House, Stokely Carmichael, Courtland Cox, Leroy Jones, Percy Johnson, Laurence Henry, Michael Thelwell, and a host of other activists responded.

Reflections on Frazier's Ideas

Let me turn now to a more specific discussion of Frazier's ideas and how Frazier's intellectual work made a contribution that's of some great importance in understanding the way the black community functioned in the past and the way the black community has functioned today.

Frazier was born in Baltimore, Maryland. He completed his education in the Baltimore public schools and enrolled at Howard in 1912, on the eve of World War I, and graduated with a B.A. (cum laude). In 1920, he attended Clark University in Worcester, Massachusetts, and in 1931 received a Ph.D. in sociology from the University of Chicago. His teaching career began at Tuskegee, where he made connections with Booker T. Washington and Robert Park. He then moved to St. Paul's Normal and Industrial School in Virginia. After that he taught at Baltimore High School for a couple of years and then moved to Morehouse College for five years, becoming director of the Atlanta School of Social Work for three years. Later he was professor in the department of sociology at Fisk, leaving there to return to Howard, where he spent the last twenty-five years of his life with visiting professorships here and there. Frazier wrote ten books, which are still worthy of study. He also wrote eighteen chapters in books, eighty-nine articles, a pamphlet, and five unpublished manuscripts. All the time, of course, he was teaching the full load required of the faculty at Atlanta, Fisk, and at Howard. The important sidelights in Frazier's career include a running battle with Melville Herskovits as to the extent and influence of African survivals in black American culture. One of the subthemes in Frazier's writings was this nonstop, knock-down fight about the nature of the African American experience. Frazier was absolutely opposed to the view that there was anything African about African Americans. He would be just boneheaded about that. Lorenzo Turner, whose course on African culture and New World survivals I took at Roosevelt University, told of a trip to Bahia where when the drums and singing began and people started doing dances based on Yoruba dance forms, Mrs. Frazier looked up and said, that's the kind of dance we used to do in North Carolina. And Frazier said, "NO, it couldn't be," and got up and walked out of the club. Professor Turner said, "And I was left with Mrs. Frazier's company the rest of the evening." Frazier would not admit into the dialog the question of the importance of Africa and African cultural values in Afro-American life. He had an interest in Africa and was one of the founding members of the African studies program at Howard. He was not anti-Africa, he was just opposed to making too much out of African cultural influences. That attitude was an important part of how he looked at the black middle class and how he conceptualized the way black Americans should develop.

Frazier was a socialist most of his life. He formed a socialist club at Howard when he was an undergraduate, a branch of the international socialist student group of which he was the president. He was one of the founding editors of *Science and Society* magazine and published in *Modern Quarterly,* both socialist journals. And throughout his life he drew upon the insights of Marxism. You cannot understand Frazier's work unless you see that Robert Park was fighting this tendency. Park was trying to impose his more static sociological categories on Frazier, but Frazier always saw himself as a radical.

Of his work on the middle class, early in his career Frazier wrote an extremely perceptive article entitled "La Bourgeoisie Noire," published in 1929 in V. F. Calverton's *Anthology of American Negro Literature.* In this article Frazier offers a brief sketch of the necessary elements of a black social *philosophy.* The article explicitly addresses the alleged failure of American Negroes to seek alliances with "left wing" groups, and it presents some of the cultural, political, and economic problems facing the black community in America. This was at the end of the 1920s. First Frazier rebuts the popular views of black Americans as different from any other ethnic groups and as uniformly lower class in status and outlook. Some black people's feelings of superiority not only to other blacks but to poor whites as well, Frazier saw, effectively barred development of empathy between and within the various groups. Race consciousness has consistently effaced class feeling among Negroes; therefore, we hear on every hand Negro capitalists supporting the right of the Negro worker to organize against white capitalists, but, nevertheless, class consciousness has never been absent. Frazier was very perceptive about this early on in his career. Many of the ideas in *Black Bourgeoisie* had been in Frazier's head for three decades before they appeared in that final form. Frazier also realized the need for a careful study and definition of the black experience in America and lamented the fact that "the civilized classes among Negroes did not have a strong economic base within the group." For this reason the Negro educated class could not be expected to embrace radical doctrines or programs that would jeopardize its existence. Frazier credited Marcus Garvey with at least attempting an economic program and credited Booker T. Washington with seeking "to place the culture of the Negro upon a sound basis by making him an efficient industrial worker." But he criticized the New Negro movement, of which he himself was a part, because it looked askance at the new rising class of black capitalism while its members basked in the sun of white capitalism. It enjoyed the congenial company of white radicals while shunning association with black radicals. Frazier felt that the New Negro movement functioned in the third dimension of culture but knew nothing of the other two dimensions—work and wealth. Frazier was beginning then to develop an analysis that linked the different segments of the black experience in a program for the liberation of the black population.

Why does Frazier rely on the black middle class? Let me point out a slippage here in the way Frazier uses his terms. When writers talk about the black middle class, in a lot of cases what they are really talking about are black intellectuals. Not all black intellectuals are necessarily middle class, nor are all the members of the black middle class intellectuals. The black middle class includes merchants, professionals, skilled workers, and so forth, all of whom work in areas that don't involve the intellectual activity that Frazier laments. A lot of Frazier's critique of intellectuals is generalized into a critique of the black middle class as a whole. And there was a tremendous amount of slippage back and forth between those terms in Frazier's time, and in the way we use those terms today. So for example, college-trained black intellectuals would be criticized for being middle class when in fact they actually were being criticized for being intellectuals. If they were working class they would still be criticized. Class was not the problem. The problem was what they did with their intellectual work. In whose service were they putting their ideas? And that may be a function of class, but not necessarily so. There is not a one-to-one correlation between a critique of the black intelligentsia and a critique of the black middle class. When Frazier talked about class, he was using Marxian terms as best he could. But he was trained as a sociologist so that status categories like middle class—which in fact is not a Marxian category—produced this conceptual confusion that made his arguments hard to follow. In any case, Frazier at this earlier point in his life was looking toward the old Negro middle class, the budding Negro capitalist class, and a budding Negro intelligentsia to provide leadership and guidance to the race. Frazier's early outlook on this was quite optimistic. In his article in Alain Locke's *The New Negro,* "Durham: The Capital of the Black Middle Class," Frazier praised the development of a

Negro capitalist class and included Negro businessmen in his definition of the New Negro movement. The essay was quite sympathetic to Negro business, quite sympathetic to the development of capitalism among black people, and quite optimistic that blacks would develop a capitalist class. In 1932, however, with the onset of the depression, Frazier was somewhat skeptical of the extent to which the new urban black middle classes were adopting the bourgeois values and behavior patterns of white society. The values of the old black middle class, which had an obligation to look after the race, were not being maintained nor was the new middle class prepared to share and support the deepening race consciousness stimulated by the Garvey movement. Frazier suggested that absence of traditions growing out of occupational status to sustain and enrich the family traditions of these families which had risen above the masses had been a weak point in the whole social structure of Negro society. The standards of the upper class had been taken over as far as possible from wealthy whites. There had been an intense struggle of the members of the class to maintain the standards of living prescribed by the comparatively wealthy few among them. Now this was the beginning of Frazier's attack on materialism and conspicuous consumption: the hedonistic, wasteful consumption among the black upper classes. Frazier wanted the black middle class to be a leadership class with a responsibility toward the black masses. However Frazier saw members of the middle class taking their money and spending it on themselves. They were frittering their opportunites away. Early on, he began to see that this was not the way to go.

Of course from a strictly Marxist point of view there was absolutely no expectation that the capitalist class would help anybody but itself. There's not a single line in Karl Marx anywhere that says that the bourgeoisie is supposed to help the proletariat. That would be against their class interest. So why would Frazier expect a Negro bourgeoisie to help a Negro proletariat? Why should the black middle class be unlike any other middle class under capitalism (i.e., selfish, greedy, and grasping)? If Frazier were a true Marxist he would have dismissed them as a frivolous group of parasites and have advocated that the black working class organize to overthrow them with the rest of the bourgeoisie. But Frazier was not a straight Marxist; he was a black Marxist living in the United States. The only source of leadership he could see, given the nature of racial oppression, was the black middle class. So, he had to search for a way to make it conscious of its obligation even though there was no structural reason why it should be. Frazier was appealing to race consciousness within the framework of Marxism. He also was hampered by the reality that many in the middle class were industrial workers. All of which makes for a very confusing analysis. Frazier's work is full of these kinds of contradictions. From a straight Marxist point of view there was no basis for criticizing the black middle class; it was the bourgeoisie. Leave it and go on to something else. But he kept coming back to it time and time again.

In his chapter "The Brown Middle Class," in *The Negro Family in the United States* (1939), we had already seen his concern with skin color. In words that were repeated again and again until they reached a shrill climax in *Black Bourgeoisie,* Frazier berates the banality and uselessness of the brown middle class. And he says, "The brown middle class that is coming into being has sloughed off in many cases the traditions of mulatto families as well as the folk culture of the masses." Personal achievement in the way of often meager educational achievements and economic success is becoming the chief requirement for admission into this class. There's not been sufficient time for class traditions to be built up, and in the absence of class tradition, suggestions and imitation play an important role in the determination of behavior. In *Black Bourgeoisie,* he suggests,

> The Negro middle class spends a relatively large amount of their time and resources on social life since they possess, on the whole, only superficial culture. They spend very little time in reading or where opportunity exists in attending the theater, art galleries or public lectures. They support the same theories of government and morality as the white middle class. Negro colleges give little attention to the plays dealing with Negro folk life, but place much emphasis upon plays which appeal to middle class whites and provide fashion shows from time to time in which middle class standards are held up for emulation.

In 1940, in *Negro Youth at the Crossways,* Frazier pointed to the differences in goals between the classes within the black community. The lower classes were concerned primarily with getting good jobs while the middle and upper classes were concerned with social and political rights. Once again, Frazier offered a definition of the black experience in America in an attempt to direct the black leadership and intelligentsia to their proper field for work and study. In defining black culture Frazier again distinguishes his views from those of Melville Herskovits. To Frazier black culture is neither directly descended from African culture nor a result of inherent racial characteristics nor identical in kind but inferior in quality to white culture. Frazier says that it is a "more or less isolated social world with its own social evaluations and distinctions." Although this world is not completely isolated from the larger white world, to a great mass of Negroes it represents a large measure of the totality of social experience which has any real meaning for them. That, in fact, is a good description of my experience growing up black in Washington, D.C. White people were not of any consequence in our daily lives in ways that we could see. One could live virtually one's entire existence within the framework of a black society and not be bothered by any actions with whites that were hostile, aggressive, or anything else. Black Americans had their own schools with black principals and teachers. They played on playgrounds controlled by blacks. Blacks went to movie theaters attended by blacks—the Lincoln, the Republic, Booker T., all on U Street. They saw live entertainment at the Howard Theater, and if they wanted to go to a nightclub, they went to the Dunbar Hotel or to other nightclubs controlled by blacks. Virtually the entirety of blacks' social life was a world of black people. If you wanted to have a fancy-dress ball you went to the Kappa House. If you wanted to show off and engage in upper-class behavior one had the Jack and Jill, the Cotillion, and the Links. And of course if you wanted to lay up on the beach you went to Carr's, Sparrows, or Highland Beach, which were black-owned and black-controlled areas. In fact whites were so little in evidence in our public school that we tended to sing the national anthem—which is to say "The Star-Spangled Banner"—primarily on those occasions when we had white visitors. The rest of the time we sang "Lift Every Voice and Sing." Black children were quite startled when told that they had to learn the national anthem because the white superintendent was coming. They said they already knew it. The music teacher said, oh no, not that one. We have to learn *their* national anthem. So I mean there was no reason to try to mangle "The Star-Spangled Banner" every day when you could sing "Lift Every Voice and Sing," which everybody knew by heart. That and Howard's alma mater were what you grew up with. It was an isolated world; it was a world cut off and distinct from the larger white world. Howard University was as good as any school we considered. Of course support was given to those people who ventured out and were competing in the larger white world. Joe Louis, Thurgood Marshall, Charles Houston, and Mary McLeod Bethune were our heroes and heroines. Though it was quite isolated, it must be said that for the most part it was a comfortable world. For many, the memories of childhood, despite our confinement to a Jim Crow world, were largely happy ones, with only a few memories of racial insults.

My early interest in African American history was stimulated in part by Dorothy Porter, curator of the Moorland-Spingarn Collection at Howard University, still one of the finest collections of black research materials in the country. You could walk in and sit down in those days because few scholars knew about it. I always did my homework from junior high in the Moorland Room. I would mention Frederick Douglass, and Dorothy Porter would get an original speech or article by Frederick Douglass and bring it to you. She was glad to make it available. If I mentioned Harriet Tubman, Porter would say, yes, I've got a speech by Wendell Phillips on Harriet Tubman. You want to see it? And I could go back in the stacks, and she would open drawers and boxes and take out wonderful things. I would not trade that for an integrated education. I don't think I could have gotten that experience at a predominately white school at the undergraduate level. To this day one of my deepest regrets is not being able to attend Dunbar High School. My sister went to Dunbar. And then after 1954 they integrated the schools. I had to go to an integrated high school. My sister had a very high grade point average, was thirty-fifth or so in her class, and had to settle for a scholarship to Oberlin College. Classmates above her were beginning to be wooed in larger numbers by the Ivy League schools. Dunbar was a brilliant place. It was run by black teachers with advanced degrees who were committed to teaching high school. These advantages and disadvantages contributed to our ambivalence about living during the Jim Crow era, which Frazier captures in "Human, All Too Human: The Negroes' Vested Interest in Segregation" published in 1947 in *Survey Graphic*. I think Frazier is right. And I confess to having feelings about that vested interest, because I grew up with a vested interest in some of those institutions. And I feel bad about the decline of those institutions. And I'm quite pleased that my daughter, after growing up in Amherst, decided to go to Spelman College and that my eldest son is attending Howard University. I think sometimes you need a space of your own to grow up in before you go out to take on the larger world. So I understand Frazier's critique, but it might be more of a description than a critique in a lot of ways.

In the pertinent sections of *The Negro in the United States,* Frazier refines his analysis, noting that with the high degree of urbanization and occupational differentiation Negroes have developed a functional leadership of five types: religious, social-welfare, political, labor, and intellectual. These functional leaders are generally secular in orientation and have adopted the practices and goals of the groups which they lead. That is, a Negro labor leader thinks and acts like his white counterpart with race treated as a decidedly subordinate factor. Frazier then observes that one important result of the increasing cooperation of whites is that it has neutralized and made impossible such racial or nationalistic movements as the Marcus Garvey movement following World War I. Socioeconomic consequences of World War II are seen as progressive in terms of the modernizing process and in terms of the solution of the particular problems of the Negro. At this time in Frazier's view there appeared to be no substantial barriers preventing the full integration of the black community into the white community along class lines.

Frazier now was thinking strictly in Marxist terms—that the black working class would integrate with the white working class, the black middle class would integrate with the white middle class, and so on. Frazier, too, had been affected by the optimism of the integrationist ideology that dominated postwar thinking on race relations. On the other hand, his detailed study of Negro institutions still tends to undermine the assumption that they are in the process of dissolution. In the period between the publication of *The Negro in the United States* (1948) and that of *Black Bourgeoisie* (1957) a number of circumstances contributed to the bitterness of Frazier's writings on black middle-class leadership and the intelligentsia.

In 1951, an eighty-third birthday celebration for W. E. B. Du Bois was planned as a fund-raising event for the Council on African Affairs. Frazier served as chairman of the dinner committee. Before the dinner took place, Du Bois and several other persons associated with the Peace Information Center were indicted by the U.S. Justice Department as agents of a foreign power: the Soviet Union. Prominent Negro educators, including the president of Howard, Mordecai Johnson, withdrew their sponsorship for the dinner almost immediately. The New York hotel cancelled the reservation just four days before the dinner was to take place. As for Frazier, to quote Du Bois, "Franklin Frazier, chairman, stood firm. He said the dinner must and would go on." And a very successful dinner was held in the safety of the ghetto at Small's Paradise in Harlem. The general reaction of the black middle class to Du Bois's indictment was extremely disheartening. Du Bois himself stated rather calmly, "The intelligentsia, the talented tenth, the successful business and professional men were not for the most part outspoken in my defense. There were many and notable exceptions but as a group this class was either silent or actually antagonistic." Some even believed Du Bois was guilty, while other Negroes of intelligence and prosperity had taken on mainstream American views in their acceptance of exploitation as defensible and their practice of conspicuous consumption, which both Du Bois and Frazier opposed. They proposed to make money and spend it as they pleased. They hated communism and socialism as much as any white American. Frazier, of course, had recognized this in the intelligentsia and middle class for some time, and this abandonment of the race's leading scholar during a time of crisis was merely another straw added to the camel's back.

Beginning in the late 1940s and continuing into the 1950s throughout Africa and the West Indies, black men raised in the same colleges as black American leadership and the students of the black American intelligentsia were forming and leading mass movements with the goal of securing for their people political freedom and self-determination. No such movement existed in the United States. Black leadership was almost completely taken in by the rash of favorable court decisions and hoped for a peaceful and rapid dissolution of segregated institutions and increased job opportunities for the middle class. In a paper delivered at Howard in April 1955, Frazier outlined the reasons for his increasing disgust with "The New Negro Middle Class." *Bourgeoisie Noire* was published in Paris later that year. In 1957 *Black Bourgeoisie* was published in English. (When Frazier's book was published in French, everybody at Howard heard about it. Frazier put a copy of the book, in French, in

Howard's library. Interested parties, of course, rushed over to read it. The joke was—and Frazier knew it was a joke—that Frazier would say, how did you like my book? And of course he got all manner of vague responses, such as, "Chapter two was just wonderful." Frazier would laugh and say these people call themselves intellectuals? They barely know English. How could they possibly read a book in French? Mordecai Johnson denounced the book at a faculty meeting and Frazier demanded to know how he could denounce it when he couldn't possibly have read it.)

In *Black Bourgeoisie* Frazier indicted virtually every aspect of Negro middle class life by contrasting the world of reality with its world of make-believe. Frazier's most important conclusions are that "because of its struggle to gain acceptance by whites, the black bourgeoisie has failed to play the role of a responsible elite in the black community. And as the intellectual leaders of the Negro community they have never dared to think beyond a narrow opportunistic philosophy that provided a rationalization for their own advantages." The work also recapitulates Frazier's view on black culture.

Frazier took the intelligentsia and leadership to task even more severely in an article "What Can the American Negro Contribute to the Social Development of Africa" published in the *Presence Africaine* volume *Africa Seen by American Negroes* (1958). Frazier's tone was so harsh that the editor of the volume, John A. Davis, felt it necessary to attempt to rebut and modify Frazier's conclusions in the introduction to the volume. Given the context of the emerging nations and the "winds of change," Frazier's charges of utter failure by the black American elite were particularly devastating. Frazier's remarks in the areas of economics, politics, intellectual leadership, and moral and spiritual leadership implicitly and explicitly belied the myth prevalent at the time that integration was taking place effectively and called once again for a rigorous evaluation of the black experience. This article could be read as a warning to Africans not to rely on their black brothers in the United States if they wanted to be liberated.

Frazier also calls Negro business a myth, suggesting that Negroes had neither the capital nor the trained managerial and technical personnel to help themselves, much less help Africa. On political development, Frazier says, "even during their greatest participation in American politics—reconstruction—Negroes did not sit in the highest councils of the nation where policies are determined." He says that Africans in their long struggle for power had acquired greater experience and some sense of responsibility. The intellectual leadership of black Americans has always been at best ambivalent toward its African origins or even its identity as Negro, preferring to consider itself American. Even more distressing to Frazier was the fact that "the Negro intellectuals in the United States have never developed a philosophy as to the meaning of human existence or a social philosophy concerning the world." Most function in a "crude philosophy of opportunism and have expressed little interest in the important changes taking place in the world around them." Frazier concludes with an anecdote: when one African intellectual was asked what he thought of a group of American Negro intellectuals, he answered he thought they were asleep.

Frazier goes on to state that as for moral and spiritual leadership and possible cultural contributions, the black American's heritage of being taken seriously has not hampered him from taking himself seriously. The reason is that black Americans have never been free—physically, psychologically, spiritually, or intellectually. The influence of the middle classes has further confused the question of cultural identification whereby insisting only upon being Americans they have become nobody. The values gaining ascendancy in Africa are those of antiracism, anticolonialism, and antiexploitation. The black middle class seeks only to share in the exploitation carried on by the United States. Therefore, Africa has little to gain morally or spiritually from an influx of black Americans—from the middle class. The prospect for a future shift in attitude, Frazier says, is dim, for as integration increases, however slowly, the black community tends to lose its identity, thereby undermining the social basis for a new cultural orientation toward Africa. Frazier concludes that as far as the contribution of black intellectuals to Africa is concerned

> they live in a world of make believe and reject identification with the cultural traditions of American Negroes as well as the African origin. They seek acceptance by white Americans at the price of losing all their racial and cultural identity, and are being swallowed up in white America. Their attitude toward the future is that of them who cried "Hail Caesar. We who are gladiators and slaves in the Roman Empire and are about to die salute you."

In his final book, *The Negro Church in America* (1964), Frazier recapitulates his criticisms of the intelligentsia and middle class, but here he concludes that perhaps integration might be the best solution after all since it would result in breaking the grip of the more backward religious leaders and would help end a mental stagnation of black intellectuals. One can see, then, that Frazier, throughout his writing, has attempted to offer an analysis of the black experience which contains all of the elements of a social philosophy from which could emanate appropriate strategies and progress, programs for the liberation of black people in the United States. His criticism of the Negro elite, and of the new black middle class of which they are a part, indicates his belief that in the context of Western and non-Western cultures and civilization it is the modernized elite and upper classes who have the responsibility for leading the entire people into the modern world. (This is not Marxism.) The black bourgeoisie in the United States has consistently failed to understand, to acknowledge, and to accept this responsibility.

In conclusion, what one sees in terms of what has happened since Frazier's *Black Bourgeoisie* is that Frazier is wrong. Black Americans did, in the middle of the integration movement, turn back to their African heritage. They did reject running whole hog into Western civilization. It's again the black American middle class, in the persons of people like Randall Robinson and several of my fellow contributors to this volume, who have maintained a consistent serious interest in Africa and African independence and who have been a great help, given the weakness of our politics in this country, in changing American policy as best they can toward the African continent. So if we look at Frazier as a warning, you can see that if you want to see what not to do, read Frazier's descriptions of what he thinks black people are doing. And if you read the history of black Americans since 1964, through the civil rights and black power movements, you will see a virtual repudiation in significant, intellectual, cultural, and political ways of the middle-class hedonism that Frazier so lamented. And the constant talk now among black intellectuals is of their responsibility and what their responsibility should be. And I don't think you'll find a single member of the black intelligentsia in any field who will not acknowledge that he or she has had some contact in some relationship to the larger black population and shares its experience in values and its responsibility.

So Frazier, I think, should be looked at and rewarded for writing something to keep us on the track; *Black Bourgeoisie* is a jeremiad, it's not his best sociological work. But it wasn't written to be. It was given a prize because the sociological establishment had failed to give him prizes for his more substantive works. So probably feeling a bit guilty, they rewarded him for *Black Bourgeoisie.* But it's a book that can be read with profit even today. If you find yourself sliding over into too many of those cocktail parties and buying too many pairs of Gucci shoes, read *Black Bourgeoisie* and get yourself back together because that's what Frazier would have wanted, and E. Franklin Frazier, for all his shortcomings, still was a wise man.

The Middle-Class Black Male

A Barometer of the Well-Being of African American Communities

WORNIE L. REED

The theme of the symposium for which this essay was originally written, "The Middle-Class Black Male: Is He Invisible?" invited a number of ways to consider the status and role of middle-class black males in American society, in general, and African American communities, in particular. Although the symposium also considered E. Franklin Frazier and his classic work *Black Bourgeoisie,* the question of the invisibility of middle-class black males raised issues that might be considered independently of the *Black Bourgeoisie* arguments. Frazier was concerned about the well-being of African American communities, which are dependent upon a viable middle class. His critique questioned the black middle class's viability or at least its orientation. Rather than critique the values and behaviors of middle-class black males, we will address the viability issue from another angle—why there are not more middle-class black males and why this matters. Not surprisingly, a smaller proportion of black men than white men have middle-class incomes, and, contrary to popular belief, the situation is not getting better. In 1995 only 85 percent of African American men had *any* income, compared to nearly 95 percent (94.7 percent) of white men, down from 88 percent and 96 percent, respectively, in 1988.[1]

Frazier chronicled the development of the black middle class in America and criticized it for overplaying, or exaggerating, itself. However, implicit in his critique was the suggestion of the

1. U.S. Bureau of the Census, *Statistical Abstract of the United States: 1998,* 118th ed. (Washington, D.C.: U.S. Government Printing Office, 1998).

importance of this developing middle class to racial progress. The middle-class status of African American families was dependent upon the black male (and often his working spouse as well).

In this essay, African American males, in general, and middle-class African American males, in particular, are assumed to be critical components of viable black communities. They are important in the building, maintenance, and sustenance of the social infrastructures of communities. Many African American communities are beset by a number of social problems, some of which could be alleviated, at least to some degree, if the communities were stronger social and economic entities. Middle-class individuals and families are integral parts of such communities.

One way of looking at Frazier's *Black Bourgeosie* is to see it as a plea for the black middle class to pursue a more solid economic base—for the ultimate benefits to African Americans and to the society at large. I am suggesting that situations and events are conspiring to make that pursuit more problematic because the existence as well as the development of middle-class men is still problematic.

The importance of middle-class African American men is implicit, if not explicit, in the work of a number of noted scholars of African American communities. St. Clair Drake and Horace Cayton in *Black Metropolis* noted that black middle-class life in "Bronzeville" mandated stable patterns of sex and family life. Working-class families were included in this formulation if they exhibited these traits. Bart Landry showed the importance of two incomes for middle-class status in the black community. William Wilson addressed what happens when men are not in the families, and in *When Work Disappears* he showed the negative effects, not only on families, but also on communities, when working-class as well as middle-class men are in short supply.[2]

To point out current problems I will briefly examine the relationship between the status of the middle-class black male and the strength of the community infrastructure, trends in the growth of middle-class black males, and factors that inhibit the development of middle-class black males.

2. Drake and Cayton, *Black Metropolis;* Landry, *New Black Middle Class;* William Julius Wilson, *The Truly Disadvantaged: The Inner City, the Underclass, and Public Policy* (Chicago: University of Chicago Press, 1987); William Julius Wilson, *When Work Disappears: The World of the New Urban Poor* (New York: Knopf, 1996).

Self-Help

There is currently widespread debate about the relative merits of self-help and government aid as viable strategies for improving the social and economic conditions of African American communities. In the long historical view, the welfare of African American communities has depended substantially on internal "self-help" organizations and activities. The question of self-improvement has faced African Americans consistently since the time of slavery. In fact, Du Bois noted a question that had been asked of African Americans less than three decades after emancipation, "It is often asked, 'What is the Negro doing to help himself after a quarter century of outside aid?' "[3]

Du Bois conducted a large-scale survey of black self-help organizations, "Some Efforts of American Negroes for Their Own Social Betterment." The research findings and proceedings of that gathering were published in 1909 as the third volume in the Atlanta University publication series. This monograph revealed that African Americans had a distinguished tradition of self-help, especially among free blacks in the North and South, during and after 250 years of slavery.

Nongovernment support systems serve as mediating structures to help individuals and families cope with and counteract adverse social forces and social policies. These mediating structures include both formal organizations (such as churches, private schools, voluntary associations) and informal systems (such as social clubs, neighborhood groups, peers, friends, and extended family networks). These organizations and systems are determined to a large extent by the social and economic status of some of the community members.[4] The social and economic status of members of the community is

3. Alfred J. Kutzik, "American Social Provision for the Aged: An Historical Perspective," in *Ethnicity and Aging: Theory, Research, and Policy,* ed. D. E. Gelfand and Alfred J. Kutzik (New York: Springer Publishing, 1979), 32–65; John S. Butler, *Entrepreneurship and Self-Help among Black Americans* (Albany, N.Y.: SUNY Press, 1991); William E. B. Du Bois, *Some Efforts of American Negroes for Their Own Social Betterment,* 1898, 4. [Online]. http://docsouth.unc.ed/church/duboisau/dubois.html [May 10, 2001].

4. William E. B. Du Bois, *The Philadelphia Negro* (1899, reprint, New York: Schocken Books, 1967); Drake and Cayton, *Black Metropolis;* Landry, *New Black Middle Class.*

crucial to the success of such self-help. And, as will be discussed below, the social and economic status of members of African American communities is highly correlated with the presence of middle-class men.

Economic Trends

Contrary to popular opinion, in terms of income, there has not been substantial growth in the relative size of the black middle class since the 1960s. However, between 1970 and 1996 the *number* of African American families with incomes between $25,000 and $49,999—the range often used to designate middle-class income—increased from 1,655,808 to 2,489,000 families, an increase of 50 percent. In fact, the absolute number of families in *each* income class increased. However, this increase in the number of black families with middle-class incomes did not keep pace with the growth in the overall number of families, which increased 71.5 percent during this 26-year period. As shown in table 1, the proportion of African American families in this middle-class income category actually *decreased* between 1970 and 1996, from 33.6 percent to 29.4 percent of all families.[5]

It is clear, as shown in table 1, that the proportion of African American families in the upper-middle-class and upper-class income ranges (over $50,000 and over $75,000) increased substantially —from 13.5 percent to 23.4 percent and from 3.2 percent to 9.0 percent, respectively. However, they constitute a relatively small proportion of all families, smaller than the proportion in the middle-class income range and smaller than the proportion of families living below the poverty level—earning less than $15,000 per year. Table 1 also compares the distribution of black family incomes to the distribution of income among white families: black family incomes tend toward the lower income ranges, and white family incomes tend toward the high income ranges.

We have seen a widening rather than a closing of the black-white income gap. Between 1970 and 1996 the ratio of black-to-white family income fell from 61.3 percent to 59.2 percent.[6] Historically, African

5. U.S. Bureau of the Census, *Statistical Abstract: 1998.*
6. Ibid.

Table 1
Money Income of Families—Percent Distribution by Income Level Black Families, U.S., in Constant (1996) Dollars: 1970–1996

	Percent Distribution by Year							
	1970	1975	1980	1985	1990	1995	1996	
							Blacks	Whites
<$10,000	17.9	17.1	18.3	20.4	20.8	18.8	18.9	5.9
$10,000 – 14,999	12.3	13.6	13.1	11.6	11.2	10.6	10.7	5.4
$15,000 – 24,999	22.8	20.3	20.5	19.5	17.0	18.0	17.6	13.0
$25,000 – 34,999	16.8	17.5	14.3	13.9	13.5	14.3	14.3	13.5
$35,000 – 49,999	16.8	16.4	16.4	15.4	15.8	16.1	15.1	18.3
$50,000 – 74,999	10.3	11.7	12.6	13.1	13.3	13.4	14.4	22.3
$75,000 +	3.2	3.5	4.9	6.3	8.3	8.6	9.0	21.7

SOURCE: U.S. Bureau of the Census, *Statistical Abstract of the United States*: 1998 (118th edition.) Washington, D.C. 1998

American families have had a higher proportion of two-earner couples than white families. However, during the 1980s and early 1990s there was a reversal of this pattern; while the proportion of all-black families with husbands and wives both working fell from 27.5 percent to 24.4 percent between 1980 and 1993, the proportion of white families with husbands and wives working rose from 32 percent to 38.8 percent.[7]

One factor contributing to this decline among African American families is the decline in married-couple families, and a significant factor in the worsening economic position of black families has been the increase in female-headed households. Between 1970 and 1995, the proportion of families headed by African American females

7. U.S. Bureau of the Census, *Statistical Abstract of the United States: 1995*, 115th ed. (Washington, D.C.: U.S. Government Printing Office, 1995).

jumped from 28 to 47 percent.[8] Although the number of female-headed families with children increased slightly less among blacks than among whites, according to Louise Hornor, blacks have more than three times as many female-headed families as whites.

Several propositions have been offered to explain the high rate of single motherhood in African American families. One of the more prominent theories was proposed by Daniel Patrick Moynihan.[9] In 1965 Moynihan, then a U.S. Department of Labor official and later a U.S. Senator from New York, described the African American family as a "tangle of pathology" and argued that a primary cause was the matriarchal nature and structure of African American families. He suggested that deterioration of the family was at the heart of the deterioration of African American communities. Black men (proportionately) had no stability in black families. Consequently, they could not be strong husbands and fathers, and black women were forced to assume the task of rearing children without men in the families.

In Moynihan's formulation, the matriarchal nature of the African American family structure resulted from American slavery, which had devastated black families. Unlike slaves in many other countries, slaves in the United States could not be legally married. As a result of this lack of legal recognition—according to Moynihan—marriage was not a strong part of the culture of blacks during or after slavery. Rather, the black family tended to be matriarchal—with reversed roles of husband and wife. Because this type of family structure was so out of line with the rest of American society, according to Moynihan, it retarded the progress of blacks as a group and led to the tangle of pathology. Because Moynihan emphasized family structure as the problem, many proposed solutions were aimed at strengthening the black family.

The decline in African American two-parent families, however, is not the result of some mystical cultural trend (i.e., black matriarchy). It is the result of forces in the mid-twentieth century, not slavery

8. Robert B. Hill et al., *Research on the African-American Family: A Holistic Perspective* (Westport, Conn.: Auburn House, 1993); Louise L. Hornor, *Black Americans: A Statistical Sourcebook* (Palo Alto, Calif.: Information Publishers, 1998).

9. Daniel P. Moynihan, "The Negro Family: The Case for National Action," in *The Moynihan Report and the Politics of Controversy*, ed. Lee Rainwater and William L. Yancey (Cambridge, Mass.: M.I.T. Press, 1967), 39–124.

Figure 1
Percent Two-Parent Families by Race, U.S., Selected Years, 1890–1995

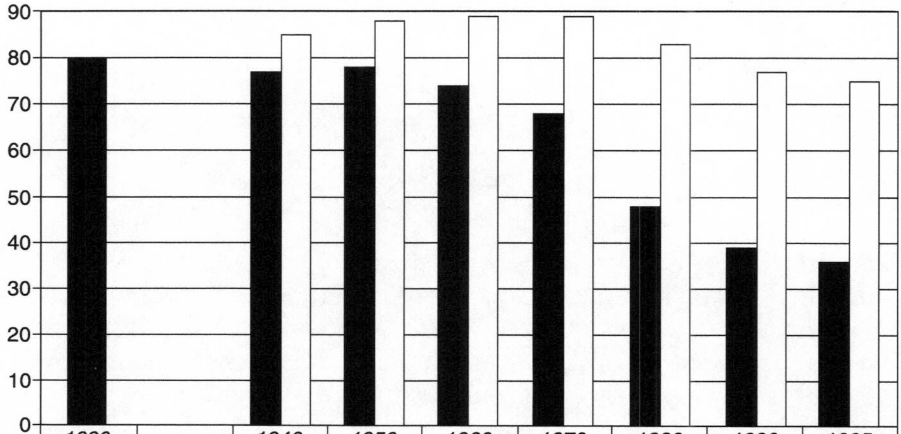

	1890		1940	1950	1960	1970	1980	1990	1995
■ Black	80		77	78	74	68	48	39	36
□ White			85	88	89	89	83	77	75

SOURCE: U.S. Bureau of the Census

or age-old culture. If slavery and culture were the causative factors, the proportion of African American households headed by women would have always been low. See figure 1, which shows that two-parent families were the rule among African Americans until after 1960, at which point the proportion of African American families with two parents begins a rather significant drop. Thus, the growth in black households headed by lone females is the result not of slavery but of more contemporary forces, not the least of which is the economic alienation of black men.[10] There is a strong correlation between the black male unemployment rate and the increase in black female-headed families (see table 2 and figure 2). As the black male unemployment rate increased between the mid-1960s and the mid-1990s and as more black males stopped looking for work altogether, the percentage of black female-headed families rose.

The decline in African American two-parent families is the result of multiple forces, the most important of which might be the

10. Wilson, *Truly Disadvantaged.*

Table 2
Black Male Unemployment, Labor Force Participation, and Black Female-Headed Families, 1960 to 1996

	Male Unemployment Rate (%)	Unemployed Plus Out of Labor Force (in millions)	Present Female-Headed Families[a]
1960	10.7	1.31	20
1965	7.4	1.45	n.a.
1970	7.3	1.77	33
1975	13.6	2.78	44
1980	14.5	3.15	49
1985	15.3	3.60	50
1990	11.3	3.62	56
1996	11.1	4.12	58

[a] Among all black families with children

n.a. Not available

SOURCES: Center for the Study of Social Policy. (1986). "The Flip-Side of Black Families Headed by Women: The Economic Status of Black Men." In R. Staples (Ed.), *The Black Family: Essays and Studies*. Belmont, CA: Wadsworth, Inc.; Horton, C.P. & Smith, J.C. (Eds.). (1990). *Statistical Record of Black America*. Detroit: Gale Research, Inc.; U.S. Bureau of the Census. (1998). *Statistical Abstract of the United States: 1998 (118th Edition)*. Washington, D.C.: U.S. Government Printing Office; L.L. Hornor (Ed.). (1998). *Black Americans: A Statistical Sourcebook*. Palo Alto, CA: Information Publications.

Figure 2
Percent Black Males Unemployed or Not in Labor Force and Percent Unmarried Black Female Heads of Households, U.S. 1950–1990

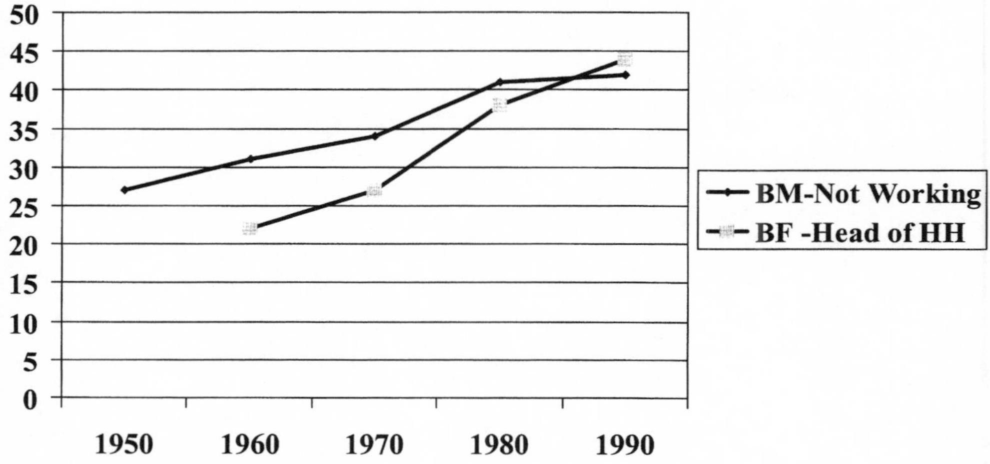

SOURCE: U.S. Bureau of the Census

economic alienation of African American men. Figure 2 shows the close correlation between the trend lines of African American male unemployment and African American female heads of household. This phenomenon has been analyzed by Wilson, William Darity, and several other investigators.[11]

Black males, in comparison with white males and black females, are failing to gain ground in middle-class status. Between 1973 and 1982 all males (white, black, and other) who were in the broad middle class maintained a 2 to 1 advantage over black males. Of course, a

11. Ibid.; William A. Darity, Jr., "Race and Inequality in the Managerial Age," in *African Americans: Essential Perspectives,* ed. Wornie L. Reed (Westport, Conn.: Auburn House, 1993), 33–80; M. Belinda Tucker and Claudia Mitchell-Kernan, "Trends in African American Family Formation," in *The Decline in Marriage among African Africans: Causes, Consequences, and Policy Implications,* ed. M. Belinda Tucker and Claudia Mitchell-Kernan (New York: Russell Sage Foundation, 1995), 3–26.

substantially higher proportion of white than black males are upper middle class.[12]

Traditionally, more black women than black men have made it into the middle class, which is just the opposite of the case among whites. Between 1973 and 1982 women, both black and white, won more of the new jobs in the broad middle class. The result was that by 1982 there were three million more white women than white men working in the broad middle class; of course, the women were not in the higher-status middle-class jobs. Black women enlarged their lead over black men, mostly through an increase in clerical jobs.

Such female-male class differences exacerbate the "marriage squeeze" presented by the excess of African American women to African American men of marriageable age.[13] One of the reasons for the increase in African American female householders is demographic: the pool of marriageable black men has been decreasing. See table 3, which shows the raw ratio of males to females since 1830. While the sex ratios among whites began to shrink after 1950, the rate among blacks had been declining for a much longer period of time. By 1990, there were only 88.2 black males for every 100 black females, while there were 96 white males for every 100 white females.

Income versus Wealth

It may be useful here to distinguish between income and wealth. All too often the economic situation of African Americans is evaluated by comparing black income to white income, which can be a mistake, as there is a much greater disparity between blacks and whites in wealth than in income.

In 1991, the median net worth of black families was approximately $4,600, while that of white families was nearly 10 times as much, approximately $44,400. In other words, for every dollar in wealth held by a white family, a comparable black family had ten

12. Landry, *New Black Middle Class.*

13. Graham B. Spanier and Paul C. Glick, "Mate Selection Differentials between Whites and Blacks in the United States," in *The Black Family: Essays and Studies*, ed. Robert Staples (Belmont, Calif.: Wadsworth, 1986), 114–28; Wilson, *Truly Disadvantaged;* Darity, "Race and Inequality," 55.

Table 3
Sex Ratios from Raw Census Data for Blacks and Whites: (U.S. 1830–1990)

Year	Blacks	Whites
1990	88.2	96.0
1980	89.6	95.3
1970	90.8	95.3
1960	93.4	97.4
1950	94.3	99.1
1940	95.0	101.2
1930	97.0	102.9
1920	99.2	104.4
1910	98.9	106.7
1900	98.6	101.5
1890	99.5	105.4
1880	97.8	104.0
1870	96.2	102.8
1860	99.6	105.3
1850	99.1	105.2
1840	99.5	104.6
1830	100.3	103.7

SOURCE: M.B. Tucker and C. Mitchell-Kernan. (1975). Marital Behavior and Expectations: Ethnic Comparisons of Attitudinal and Structural Correlates. In M.B. Tucker and C. Mitchell-Kernan, *The Decline in Marriage Among African Americans*. New York: Russell Sage Foundation.

cents. For those families with moderate incomes, the net worth of whites was more than six times that of blacks. White families with middle-class incomes have three or more times the wealth of their black counterparts.[14]

The breakdown by family type shows that white married-couple families had nearly four times more wealth than black married-couple families, and white female-headed families had nearly forty-seven times more wealth than black female-headed families. In fact, white female-headed families had, on average, greater net worth than black married-couple families.

In addition to the *extent* of asset ownership, blacks and whites also diverge when it comes to the *composition* of asset ownership. Compared with white householders, black householders held a greater percentage of their net worth in durable goods such as housing (65 versus 41 percent) and motor vehicles (11 versus 6 percent) and a lower percentage in financial assets such as stocks and mutual-fund shares (1 versus 7 percent) and deposits at financial institutions (7 versus 15 percent).[15] These data may explain the difficulty that blacks have in raising even limited amounts of capital for small business ventures or in passing their middle-class status on to their children.

The middle-class standard of living rests on both income and wealth. Wealth is necessary to make or keep the status secure. It helps safeguard the middle-class standard of living and guards against an interrupted flow of income. When viewed this way, the middle-class status of many African Americans is not very secure.

Some Factors Limiting the Black Male

Earnings Disparity

As African American men move into middle-class occupations, those occupations are returning less and less money in earnings. The

14. U.S. Bureau of the Census. *Statistical Abstract of the United States: 1994*, 114th ed. (Washington, D.C.: U. S. Government Printing Office, 1994), 482; Melvin L. Oliver and Thomas M. Shapiro, *Black Wealth/White Wealth* (New York: Routledge, 1995), 197.

15. William A. Darity, Jr., and Samuel L. Myers, Jr., "Family Structure and the Marginalization of Black Men: Policy Implications," in *Decline in Marriage among African Africans*, ed. M. Belinda Tucker and Claudia Mitchell-Kernan, 263–308.

disparity in the earnings of blacks and whites in upper-level white-collar occupations is greater than that between their counterparts in blue-collar occupations. There has been growth in the proportion of the black male workforce in white-collar occupations. In fact, between 1959 and 1987, the proportion nearly doubled, from 15.2 percent to 28.6 percent. However, in 1979 black males in upper-level white-collar occupations earned less on average relative to white males than did their blue-collar counterparts. The black male/white male earnings ratio was seventy-one cents for every dollar among white-collar occupations and seventy-nine cents for every dollar among blue-collar occupations. These differences persist when educational level is controlled. For example, among executives and administrators in 1979, the black male/white male earnings ratio for individuals with a four-year college education was sixty-two cents for every dollar.[16]

Shifts in Labor Markets

Between 1940 and 1975 manufacturing jobs, which traditionally paid high wages to male workers with low skill levels, were a major means for African American families to move up into the middle-income bracket. However, the national shift from a manufacturing to a service economy has had adverse effects on current and future prospects for African American workers. Predictably, black employment fell considerably faster during the 1980s than overall employment in most of the affected industries. This shift away from manufacturing has produced what some analysts call a skills mismatch for low-skilled African American males.[17]

There is also the issue of spatial mismatch, resulting from the relocation of industries from the cities, where most African Americans

16. Jeremiah P. Cotton, "Recent Changes in the Structure and Value of African-American Male Occupations," *Trotter Institute Review* 4, 3:6–11 (Boston: University of Massachusetts at Boston, William Monroe Trotter Institute, 1990).

17. Wilson, *Truly Disadvantaged;* James H. Johnson and Melvin L. Oliver, "Structural Changes in the U.S. Economy and Black Male Joblessness: A Reassessment," in *Urban Labor Markets and Job Opportunity,* ed. George E. Peterson and Wayne Vroman (Washington, D.C.: Urban Institute Press, 1992), 113–47; Margaret C. Simms, *Black Economic Progress: An Agenda for the 1990s* (Washington, D.C.: Joint Center for Political Studies, 1988); Arnold H. Packer and John G. Wirt, "Changing Skills in the U.S. Workforce: Trends of Supply and Demand," in *Urban Labor Markets and Job Opportunity,* 31–65.

live, to suburban areas. Harry Holzer and Wayne Vroman found that approximately one-third of the difference across metropolitan areas in the change in labor force participation rates for African Americans in the 1970s was due to manufacturing job loss.[18]

Racial Discrimination in Schooling and Hiring

We should not overlook the continuing effects of racial discrimination on the economic prospects for African American males. Gary Orfield cites urban schooling as a culprit in the "perpetuation of job inequality."[19] He sees spatial mismatches in educational resources as well as the location of jobs. "Teachers and counselors are distributed in ways that reinforce inequality. There are long-standing patterns of concentrating the best-qualified teachers from the most competitive colleges in the schools with the most affuent and high-achieving students."

Economist and former Federal Reserve Board member Andrew Brimmer has been tracking the economic cost of discrimination against African Americans since the 1960s.[20] He has shown that the American economy lost between 1.5 and 2.2 percent of the gross national product (GNP) yearly from 1967 to 1993 because of racial discrimination against African Americans that limited the full use of their existing education.

In 1967 this loss amounted to 1.5 percent of the GNP, or $12.1 billion. By 1993 it had grown to 2.2 percent of the GNP, $137.5 billion. When the cost of the failure to improve and fully utilize the education of African Americans is considered, another 1.4 percent of the GNP is lost in 1967. A total of 2.9 percent of the GNP, $23.2 billion, was lost to the American economy in 1967. By 1993 this proportion of lost GNP had grown to 3.8 percent of the GNP, $240.9 billion. Thus, racial discrimination costs the economy as well as individual African American families and communities.

18. Harry J. Holzer and Wayne Vroman, "Mismatches and the Urban Labor Market," in *Urban Labor Markets and Job Opportunity*, 81–112.

19. Gary Orfield, "Urban Schooling and the Perpetuation of Job Inequality in Metropolitan Chicago," in *Urban Labor Markets and Job Opportunity*, 161–99.

20. Andrew Brimmer, "The Economic Cost of Discrimination against Black Americans," in *Economic Perspectives on Affirmative Action*, ed. Margaret C. Simms (Washington, D.C.: Joint Center for Political and Economic Studies, 1995), 9–30.

The Role of the Middle-Class Black Male in Community Development

While we have concern and interest in the improvement of the welfare of the middle-class black male and the concomitant growth of the black middle class, the key concern here is on the potential for community development (i.e., improvement as a result of the enhancement of middle-class African Americans).

Some scholars argue that this should be accomplished by a kind of updated entrepreneurial effort, an effort that could develop from new or revitalized voluntary associations within black communities that would have specific orientations toward business development.[21] It is assumed that increases in the numbers of middle-class males—and their families—in black communities, participating in its organizations and institutions, will have the effect of generating some kind of positive community development. Another assumption of this analysis is that the development of African American communities will not result from changes forced upon its economic life from the outside. Rather, changes will come about from self-directed initiatives. This self-help will depend upon having the wherewithal to develop and manage such efforts. Presumably this requires middle-class families.

Conclusions

I have suggested that many of the problems that African American communities confront are adversely affected by the declining economic status of African American men. Their economic status affects familial situations as well as the general community infrastructure. Perhaps some of the attention that is paid to poor female-headed households should be given to halting the increasing economic alienation of black men. Any turnaround in this trend would have the effect of increasing the numbers of black middle-class males and middle-class families, which might affect in a positive manner the quality of life in urban black communities.

21. Shelly Green and Paul Pryde, *Black Entrepreneurship in America* (New Brunswick, N.J.: Transaction Publishers, 1990).

Some readers may question how an increase in the number of middle-class African American males, and therefore middle-class families, could be the route to improving African American communities, especially those in urban areas, as middle-class blacks are moving to the suburbs—away from such communities. Evidence indicates, however, that the residential segregation of African Americans is still high. Between 1950 and 1970, blacks in neighborhoods in twenty large cities, where they represented three-fourths of the population, increased from 30 to 51 percent, while the proportion of blacks in mixed neighborhoods with 25 percent or fewer blacks declined from 25 percent to 16 percent. Further, the overall national black segregation index—the degree of racially segregated housing in the United States—decreased only minutely between 1940 and 1990, from 85.2 to 81.[22] Thus, the majority of blacks still live in mostly black neighborhoods. Consequently, strengthening the black middle class should inevitably strengthen black communities. And this can be done by increasing the numbers of middle-class males.

It is interesting to imagine a Frazier critique of the black middle class today. If it took the same approach as *Black Bourgeoisie,* it is likely that among other issues Frazier would chide the black middle class for not paying more attention to the threats to the growth in their numbers suggested above.

22. Wornie L. Reed, *Minorities in Ohio: Trends and Projections, Chart Essay* (Cleveland: Cleveland State University, Urban Child Research Center, 1998).

E. Franklin Frazier's *Black Bourgeoisie* Reconsidered

Frazier's Analytical Perspective

MARTIN KILSON

It has been nearly fifty years since E. Franklin Frazier (who ranked at the top of a brilliant group of first-generation African American social scientists trained in the 1920s and 1930s, such as Charles Spurgeon Johnson, Allison Davis, Horace Mann Bond, Ralph J. Bunche, John Aubrey Davis, and St. Clair Drake) published his book *Black Bourgeoisie.* By the time of Frazier's death in 1962, the economic and political groundwork were in place for growth of the American middle class and professional sector (what Frazier dubbed "la bourgeoisie noire"). Thus, the size of the black bourgeoisie today surpasses anything Frazier could have imagined; it is several times what it was when Frazier wrote his book. The dual status that the black bourgeoisie holds within the black and American settings is today infinitely more complex than it was two generations ago. What was Frazier's initial focus in his study of the black bourgeoisie? In general, Frazier's probe of the African American middle and upper strata nearly fifty years ago focused less on these strata's "power-structure dimensions" than on their "societal dimensions." He took this analytical vantage point because the racial-caste marginalization of African Americans' status in American society prevented any serious access by blacks to roles in the power structure.

Thus, inasmuch as racial caste practices rigidly marginalized black Americans and truncated their modern development, this in turn translated into a systemically distorted and dysfunctional African American subsystem within the overall modernizing

American system. To describe the distortions that characterized the twentieth-century African American subsystem, E. Franklin Frazier and other social observers of African American life used the term *social pathology.* Of course, many of the "social pathologies" associated with the racial-caste constraints on African American subsystem during the first half of the twentieth century were concentrated among the weak working class and poor majority sector of black Americans—in the form of high crime rates, intragroup or fratricidal violence, weak familial patterns, and so on. But in Frazier's analytical approach, the black middle-class and upper-class strata—the bourgeoisie—also exhibited signs of "social pathology."

In a review of Gunner Myrdal's *An American Dilemma* that appeared in the *Crisis* in 1994, Frazier formulates the social pathology conception as follows: "Myrdal recognized the Negro community for what it was—a pathological phenomenon in American life. . . . He recognized that segregation [racial caste] kept the Negro in poverty and ignorance. . . . It is not surprising then that he did not indulge in over-rating the achievements of the Negroes and the ability and character of their leaders." From this formulation it is, of course, just one small step to Frazier's rather slashing critical formulations on the character of the black bourgeoisie offered in his book of the same name. As he observes in the American edition:

> The exclusion of middle-class Negroes from [equal] participation in the general life of the American community has affected their entire outlook on life. It has meant that whites did not regard the activities of Negroes as of any real consequence in American life. It has tended to encourage a spirit of irresponsibility or an attitude of "play" or make-believe among them. Consequently, Negroes have "played" at conducting their schools, at running their businesses, and at practicing their professions. The spirit of play or make believe has tended to distort or vitiate the ends of their most serious activities. . . . Since [the members of] the black bourgeoisie live largely in a world of make-believe, the masks which they wear to play their sorry roles conceal the feelings of inferiority . . . that haunt their inner lives. . . . Their escape into a world of make believe with its sham "society" [conspicuous status-seeking] leaves them with a feeling of emptiness and futility.[1]

1. Frazier, *Black Bourgeoisie,* 169–70, 176.

Thus, looking back on the development of the African American middle-class, professional sector—the bourgeoisie—through the first fifty years of the twentieth century, E. Franklin Frazier focused on what I call its "societal dimensions." And for Frazier these "societal dimensions" exhibited mainly dysfunctional tendencies, or as he put it: "a spirit of irresponsibility or an attitude of 'play' of make-believe. . . . The spirit of play or make-believe has tended to distort or vitiate the ends of their most serious activities." Now while there is undoubtedly an element of systemic truth in Frazier's "pathology perspective" on the first fifty-year period of the black bourgeoisie, I would also argue that Frazier exaggerated the application of his "pathology perspective." His discussion of consumeristic frivolity among the black middle-class and upper strata was exaggerated, for instance, especially in the context of similar obsession with conspicuous consumption among the bourgeoisie sector in white groups, like WASPS, Irish Americans, and Jewish Americans. Similarly, though frivolous professional behavior could be found among the black middle-class and professional sector during the first fifty years of the twentieth century, frivolous professional behavior was also present among whites in the bourgeois sector. Evidence for the "social pathologies" among white ethnic groups in twentieth-century American society can be found in Andrew Greeley's studies on Irish Americans, such as his candid analysis in *That Most Distressful Nation: The Taming of the American Irish* (1972), and also in studies on the white-ethnic political class, such as Harold Foote Gosnell's *Machine Politics: Chicago Model* (1935) and Harold Zink's *Twenty Municipal Bosses* (1938).

Furthermore, for E. Franklin Frazier's discussion on this topic to be taken seriously, Frazier was, I think, obligated to produce direct evidence of specific black professionals and/or professional institutions that fell into his "pathological category." Moreover, it presumably never occurred to Frazier that there were countervailing patterns that involved high-level professional behavior among the African American middle-class and upper strata during the first fifty years of the twentieth century, and these countervailing patterns were represented broadly within the black bourgeoisie among lawyers, doctors, teachers, businesspersons, dentists, engineers, scholars like himself, and so on. Following Frazier's death in 1962, a number of studies on high-performing professionals among middle-class African Americans during the first fifty years of the twentieth century were published.[2]

In this connection, it should also be mentioned that Frazier exaggerated the role of middle-class black women as purveyors of materialistic consumerism. Frazier failed to recognize that middle-class black women performed constructively as contributors to the aggregate income of middle-class black households. From the 1920s onward they were employed outside their homes at two to three times the rate of middle-class white women.

An Overview

Within a decade of Frazier's death in 1962, sparked especially by public policies extracted from the federal government by the civil rights movement, the African American middle-class and professional sector experienced significant social mobility advances. In the first instance, between the 1960s and 1980s, there was a simultaneous growth of white-collar occupations among African Americans and a marked occupational differentiation. During the first five years of the 1960s, in fact, some 380,000 nonwhites (mainly African Americans) acquired white-collar employment, increasing the number of nonwhites in the middle-class to some four million. And by 1980 about 40 percent of working African Americans were located in white-collar jobs. This compared with 52 percent of white Americans and 32.4 percent of Latinos. There was also educational advancement of African Americans; the number of blacks graduating high school increased from 42 to 75 percent between 1960 and 1980.[3]

2. See, for example, Kenneth R. Manning, *Black Apollo of Science: The Life of Ernest Everett Just* (New York: Oxford University Press, 1983). I attempt to analytically contextualize the Frazierian issue of "play acting" and "make-believe" behavior among the twentieth-century black middle-class and professional sector in my study *The Making of Black Intellectuals: Studies on the African-American Intelligentsia* (forthcoming). My purpose is to correct the imbalance in Frazier's "social pathology" argument in *Black Bourgeoisie.*

3. Data on the growth of white-collar jobs among African Americans from the 1960s to 1980s can be found in the following: Dan Cortz, "The Negro Middle Class," *Fortune* (Nov. 1966); Richard Freeman, *Black Elite: The New Market for*

A panoramic perspective on African Americans' position in white-collar jobs is shown by data in table 1—covering the era from the end of the Great Depression in 1940 to 1980—from the National Academy of Science's major survey of the overall status of African Americans organized by Gerald Jaynes and Robin Williams in the late 1980s. Numbering about 200,000 black white-collar job holders in 1940, this category had increased to 474,060 by 1960, and by 1980 the black white-collar category had more than doubled, standing at 1,564,914.

An equally important feature of the expansion of white-collar ranks among African Americans during the post-Frazier years was that both males and females shared in this transformation. Both at the lower and upper ranks of white-collar jobs, black women strengthened their position relative to their white counterparts, more so, in fact, than did black men. For example, by 1980 some 14 percent of black women held professional/technical jobs compared to 17 percent of white women, whereas 8 percent of black males held such jobs compared to 16 percent of employed white males.

Viewed in terms of specific professional/technical occupations, by the early 1980s the female/male percentage of these occupations among African Americans had advanced significantly. Within their categories (jobs held by all women/jobs held by all men):

- Black females held 7.4 percent and black males 3.6 percent percent of accounting positions.
- Black females held 9.4 percent and black males 4.1 percent of computer specialist positions.
- Black females held 10.8 percent and black males 7.9 percent of personnel and labor specialist positions.
- Black females held 0.5 percent and black males 2.1 percent of medical and dental practitioner positions.
- Black females held 9.2 percent and black males 8.4 percent of health technician positions.
- Black females held 5.3 percent and black males 3.3 percent of college teaching positions.

Highly Educated Black Americans (New York: McGraw Hill, 1976); and Landry, *New Black Middle Class.*

Table 1
Selected White-Collar Occupations Filled by Blacks, 1940–1980

Occupation	1940 Number	(Percent)	1950		1960		1970		1980	
Managerial	62,220	(33.2)	112,020	(37.5)	121,762	(25.7)	170,035	(21.8)	487.432	(31.1)
Self-employed	49,760	(26.5)	73,560	(24.6)	63,357	(13.4)	34,893	(4.5)	21,781	(1.4)
Private salary	10,940	(5.8)	32,580	(10.9)	44,318	(9.3)	87,765	(11.2)	282,488	(18.1)
Government	1,240	(0.7)	5,250	(1.8)	12,282	(2.6)	46,388	(5.9)	181,847	(11.6)
Professional and Technical	125,330	(66.8)	186,930	(62.5)	352,298	(74.3)	611,334	(78.2)	1,077,482	(68.9)
Clergy	17,920	(9.6)	19,110	(6.4)	14,530	(3.1)	12,850	(1.6)	16,195	(1.0)
Engineers	300	(0.2)	2,730	(0.9)	12.049	(2.5)	13,679	(1.8)	36,019	(2.3)
Lawyers and judges	1,000	(0.5)	1,530	(0.5)	2,970	(0.6)	3,728	(0.5)	15,277	(1.0)
Physicians	4,160	(2.2)	4,500	(1.5)	9,983	(2.1)	6,106	(0.8)	13,509	(0.9)
Social Workers	2,270	(1.5)	6.750	(2.3)	15,345	(3.2)	40,791	(5.2)	88,512	(5.6)
Teachers	67,660	(36.0)	90,180	(30.2)	150,743	(31.8)	240,073	(30.7)	424,755	(27.1)
Totals	187,520	(100.0)	298,950	(100.0)	474,060	(100.0)	781,369	(100.0)	1,564,914	(100.0)

SOURCE: Gerald Jaynes & Robin Williams, *A Common Destiny: Blacks and American Society* (Washington, 1989) p. 170.

- Black females held 10.2 percent and black males 5.5 percent of school teaching positions.
- Black females held 12.2 percent and black males 2.6 percent of school administrative positions.
- Black females held 4.6 percent and black males 2.6 percent of banking and financial official positions.
- Black females held 6.7 percent and black males 5.6 percent of engineering and science technician positions.
- Black females held 7.1 percent and black males 3.1 percent of lawyer and judge positions.[4]

Moreover, the impact of affirmative action policies and practices persisted into the 1990s, resulting in a steady advance of middle-class and professional-level occupations among African Americans. Selected aspects of this advance are shown in table 2.

New Mainstreaming Patterns

Middle-class and professional sector employment patterns among African Americans in the post-Frazier era have shifted from

4. These data can be found in Diane Westcot, "Blacks in the 1970s," *Monthly Labor Review* (June 1982).

Table 2
Selected Middle-Class Occupations Held by Blacks, 1990
(Numbers in the Thousands)

OCCUPATIONS	U.S.TOTAL	PERCENT BLACK
Managers (marketing, management, public relations)	630	2.1
Managers (properties, real estate)	302	6.3
Computer Systems Analysts	987	5.8
Engineers	1,919	3.6
Registered Nurses	2,494	7.1
Therapists (occupational, physical)	479	7.2
Computer Programmers	882	6.7
University Teachers	846	4.8
Special Education Teachers	467	9.5
Health Technologists	2,595	12.9
Biological Scientists	83	2.0
Chemists	96	5.2
Engineering Technicians & Technologists	1,640	7.2
Accountants & Auditors	1,325	7.6
Educational/Vocational Counselors	192	15.5

SOURCE: *Black Enterprise* (February 1993) p. 67.

a black ghetto job market to nationwide job markets, including bank chains, insurance companies, rental firms, airline companies, white college campuses, chemical firms, computer businesses, a broad range of government jobs, and scientific research firms. New occupations provided by government agencies have played a role in this job-market mainstreaming process; government agencies now employ some 30 percent of white-collar black families, compared to 16 percent of white-collar white families. Sociologically, the new occupational dispersion—which was inconceivable among the middle class studied by Frazier nearly fifty years ago—affects a broad range of social relationships among the black bourgeoisie, thereby altering the historical patterns. New kinds of workplace milieus for middle-class and professional blacks afford them new social networks and cultural orientations. When those changes are reinforced, in turn, by the growing shift from residing in compact black urban communities to residing in more racially dispersed suburban communities, we have in place the preconditions for a new kind of systemic mainstreaming of the black bourgeoisie—a phenomenon that was not on the black American mobility agenda when E. Franklin Frazier wrote about the black bourgeoisie.

We have no better source for documenting the new occupational and sociocultural dispersion of the African American upper stratum than the journal *Black Enterprise,* the first black multimillion-dollar entrepreneurial magazine (circulation 250,000), owned and edited by Earl Graves. For example, in September 1975 *Black Enterprise* evaluated the degree of black penetration of the executive ranks of American foundations. Among the major foundations with African American heads have been the following: Charles Kettering Foundation, Borden Foundation, Avon Foundation, Lilly Endowment, John Hay Whitney Foundation, TRW Foundation, Josiah Macy Foundation, Twentieth Century Fund, Borg-Warner Foundation, Charles Stewart Mott Foundation, Phelps-Stokes Fund, Rockefeller Brothers Fund, Rockefeller Foundation, Ford Foundation, Cleveland Foundation, and the Chicago Foundation.

Equally noteworthy has been the black penetration of middle-level technical and managerial ranks of medium-sized and large corporations. For over twenty-five years monthly issues of *Black Enterprise* have carried a column entitled "Making It," comprising a job profile of persons exemplifying the occupational dispersion of the black bourgeoisie into mainstream corporations. In the September and October 1979 issues, the column listed the following instances of the new occupational breakthrough by the black elite:

> Hallie Anderson—promoted to supervisor of the Group Claims Division at the Phoenix Mutual Life Insurance Co. (Hartford); Bill Baker—appointed Manager of Communications for Blue Cross/Blue Shield (Colorado); Jack Bell—elected president of the Texas Restaurant Association and the first black to head his 5,500 member group; Columbus Coleman—promoted to executive vice-president and general manager of Wells Fargo Securities Clearance Corporation (New York);

> Tom Finch—formerly director of Matrix Operations for Meadowlands and Giants Stadium (New Jersey) was appointed director of Promotions at Arlington Park Race Track Corporation (Arlington Heights, IL); Jay Francis—elected vice-president of Westinghouse Broadcasting Company; Edward T. Gilliam II—appointed Internal Audit Manager at Toro Company (Minneapolis); Cresswotth Lander—appointed managing director for Civil Aeronautics Board; James Lockhart—formerly vice president of Legal Affairs at Budget Rent-a-car Corporation was appointed vice-president for Public Affairs for TransAmerica Corporation; George Brown—appointed to executive vice president at Grumman Energy Systems Inc. (Bethpage, N.Y.); Stephen Daniels—appointed manager for Reservationist Trans World Airlines (New York Region); and Aldred Fornay—appointed creative director at Revlon Corporation.

The importance of these job-market-based social-class transformations among middle-class and professional African Americans cannot be overemphasized. Such transformations free the new black bourgeoisie from a traditionally segregated job market, which had socially rigidified and politically emasculated the old black bourgeoisie, spawning the "societal pathologies" described by Frazier. In a word, these job-market transformations among middle-class and professional blacks represent an unprecedented randomization of white-collar occupations and white-collar job market regional locations for African Americans. This has meant, above all, that members of the new black bourgeoisie have access to a variety of technical and cultural networks that ultimately facilitate a new kind of systemic mainstreaming of middle-class and professional African Americans.

In general, the systemic mainstreaming of black bourgeoisie in the post-Frazier era occurs along a protracted and uneven developmental trajectory, not a straight-line trajectory. This is so not only because of the tenacity of racist sociocultural patterns among white Americans, but also because of the sway of sociocultural friendship and network patterns among African Americans. Thus in the first instance the new job-market opportunities available to middle-class and professional African Americans spawned a new range of black professional associations and, through these, a new range of black social-class networks. Among the new associational infrastructure that evolved within the post-Frazier black bourgeoisie, the following have been representative: the National Association of Black Manufacturers (founded 1971); the National Association of Black

Accountants (1970); the National Association of Black Contractors (1972); the National Black Media Coalition (1973); the National Black Network (1973); the Council of Concerned Black Executives (c. 1975); and the Organization of Black Airline Pilots (1976). Furthermore, an institutionalized African American political class of elected and appointed officeholders has evolved along with other professions in the new black bourgeoisie (with eight thousand elected and perhaps thirty thousand appointed officials), and this sector has also fashioned a network of nationwide associations. These include the National Black Caucus of State Legislators, the National Association of Minority Country Officials, and the National Caucus of Black Schoolboard Members. Moreover, the nationwide associations are reinforced at the local level (city especially) by a plethora of similar black organizations, ranging from the Dallas Alliance for Enterprise and the Burham Business and Professional Chain to New York City's influential One Hundred Black Men.

Though all black in composition like the professional associations in the pre-1960s era, the new post-Frazier era associations have a fundamentally different relationship to mainstream American bourgeois patterns. Keep in mind that pre-1960s black professional organizations, like the National Negro Business League (founded by Booker T. Washington in 1900), functioned protectively, so to speak. They shielded middle-class African American business and professional activities from the pressures of white supremacy and shored up black ghetto markets. On the other hand, the new post-Frazier era associations function integratively. They open broad job-market and professional/business opportunities for middle-class and professional African Americans throughout the American political, economic, and social systems. Put another way, even while the new black professional associations among lawyers, engineers, administrators, architects, and accountants in the post-Frazier era continued as mainly African American in membership, they now operated broadly within the mainstream American economy. They had become deghettoized, which means that operationally the members of black professional associations in the post-Frazier era interact frequently with white professionals alongside whom they work in mainstream white-owned law firms, accounting firms, computer businesses, and so on. Thus, over time, we can expect a growing proportion of middle-class and professional African Americans to acquire social and political attitudes that have also become deghettoized. That is, social and political attitudes will be influenced less by racial realities of a ghetto type, that is to say by racial realities confronting the working-class and poor sectors of African Americans. A similar shift occurred in the social and political attitudes among the middle-class sector of white ethnic groups (e.g., Irish Americans, Polish Americans, Italian Americans, Jewish Americans) when, from the 1940s through the 1960s—these groups' middle-class migrated to middle-class suburbs, leaving behind the working-class and poor sectors among white ethnic groups. Among the post–World War II white ethnic middle-class elements, a less combative attitude toward the status-dominant White-Anglo-Saxon-Protestant group emerged, and this, in turn, was reflected in more conservative, Republican-leaning voting habits. However, so far in the post-Frazier era a significant shift in voting patterns among middle-class and professional African American elements away from the Democratic party has not occurred, though I would suggest that the new job-market incorporation of black professionals on a national level will likely facilitate this kind of change in voting behavior in due course.

New Systemic Dynamics among Black Bourgeoisie

In E. Franklin Frazier's critique of the black bourgeoisie as it was in the 1950s, in addition to identifying distortions in the performance of modern middle-class and professional functions or tasks among the black bourgeoisie, Frazier also identified distortions in what might be called the "leadership thrust" or "leadership aura" of this social stratum. The black bourgeoisie's leadership aura was, in Frazier's view, rendered flaccid and directionless by too many members' indulgence in what he variously called "make-believe" or "high society" behavior, which is to say, they acted out the frivolous aspects of genuine bourgeois elite behavior, expending their limited wealth in conspicuous consumerism and a leisure style of expensive gaiety. In Frazier's view, this was the opposite of what a truly viable black bourgeoisie required as its guiding motif. Namely, it required what might be called a "power-seeking" leadership aura.

Now while there was much truth in this aspect of the Frazierian critique of middle-class and professional African Americans in the early 1950s, it is clear from our vantage point today that the revolution in civil rights laws and practices that uprooted a century of white supremacist marginalization of African Americans was a necessary precondition for correcting the leadership distortions that Frazier identified among the black bourgeoisie. Above all, it was the revolution in civil rights laws and practices that—as I have demonstrated—transformed the opportunities available to middle-class and professional blacks from a ghetto job market to a nationwide job market.

Indeed, simultaneous with this new access, African Americans fashioned new networks of professional organizations among accountants, engineers, lawyers, computer technologists, media entrepreneurs, and so on. And this new black organizational process was the beginning of a significant shift in the leadership aura of the black bourgeoisie away from the "high-society" pattern that Frazier so sharply critiqued and toward what I call a "power-mustering" bourgeois outlook. The individuals who headed up the new professional organizations viewed them overwhelmingly as power-mustering agencies in terms of technocratic, educational, and professional standing for their new job-market members as engineers, accountants, computer technologists, television owners, and media technicians.

This new power-mustering leadership aura also evolved through other modalities, especially through new African American journals. Beginning in the 1970s, the most prominent of these black journals appeared monthly and sought nationwide black readership. The journal *Black Enterprise* led the way, reaching 250,000 readers by the mid-1980s and approaching 1 million readers today. Another of these power-mustering black journals was directed mainly toward new female members among middle-class and professional African Americans. That journal was *Essence,* which by the mid-1980s had around 600,000 readers and today has well over 1 million. While *Essence* readers are offered content on fashionable clothing or interior design of upper middle-class homes, they are also informed about the new professional and business careers of successful African American women. Perhaps the biggest surprise among the new genre of black magazines that emphasize what I call power-mustering orientations has been changes in the contents of *Ebony* magazine. It is the oldest popular black magazine—started in the

1950s—and until the 1970s *Ebony* fed its black readers on a heavy diet of what E. Franklin Frazier called "high-society" orientations: articles that emphasized the consumerist lifestyles of black entertainers mainly but also of black professionals and businesspersons. Since 1970s, however, *Ebony* has increasingly given attention to the new professional and business careers among African Americans, with articles tracing the methods and processes that made these careers possible. A final category of new power-mustering black journals is represented by *Black Collegian,* which offers a vast array of articles on topics related to how black college graduates can prepare themselves to enter the mainstream job market.

It is especially in the upper-middle-class and top-level professional black households that the new power-mustering leadership aura propagated by new black journals has a major impact. For example, the journal *Black Enterprise* carries a variety of monthly columns with power-mustering titles such as "Making It," "On the Move," and "Names in the News." These columns offer brief career biographies that celebrate a preference for the power-mustering lifestyle. *Black Enterprise* also carries fuller portraits of successful black entrepreneurial figures and in-depth reports on successful black businesses, as well as numerous articles on successful financial, commercial, and corporate strategies.

The overriding goal of new power-mustering black journals has been to galvanize the systemic mainstreaming of the black bourgeoisie. And the cumulative impact of these developments is transforming the customary character of American race relations in a manner that E. Franklin Frazier, writing in the early 1950s, could not have imagined. Above all, there is emerging what might be called a status-deracialization process among the post-Frazier black bourgeoisie. To speak of status-deracialization is another way of identifying those alterations in the historical dynamics of racism in American life that William Julius Wilson has characterized as "declining significance of race." But unlike Wilson's conception, my conception of status-derecialization does not imply that racism as such has ceased to exist. Far from it. The term *status-deracialization* denotes that racism now has less capacity than two generations and more ago to dictate the systemic patterning of an expanding segment of mobile African Americans, the bourgeoisie sector especially. Today this sector among African Americans constitutes a kind of "upper stratum" made up of middle-class and professional households that amount to some 35 percent of black households. Another 25 percent of black households fall into the stable blue-collar or stable working-class sector, making up a "middle-stratum" black sector. The remaining 40 percent "lower-stratum" black sector comprises weak working-class and poor black households.

In general, the new systemic incorporating process that I call status-deracialization is likely to proceed in an erratic manner at best, characterized by breakthroughs on one front and setbacks on another. Owing to residual racist practices among white Americans, the setbacks slow down the replacement of race- and class-linked attitudes among the post-Frazier black bourgeoisie, thereby restricting the ideological range of class differentiation among African Americans. Put another way, as status-deracialization proceeds in the post-Frazier era, class perceptions and identity among the black bourgeoisie will display numerous inconsistencies. On some issues, upper-stratum blacks will converge with upper-stratum whites. On other issues however, upper-stratum blacks will converge with middle- and lower-stratum blacks and the broader African American community. Why are there such inconsistencies in the status-deracialization process?

The erratic manner by which upper-stratum African Americans are co-opted into the American mainstream in our post-Frazier era leaves them, as it were, both "insiders" and "outsiders." While processing full-fledged elite capabilities in a way that E. Franklin Frazier could not have foreseen fifty years ago, today's black bourgeoisie is still vulnerable to powerful patterns of residual racism in American life. Furthermore, the insider/outsider condition facing today's black bourgeoisie is influenced by the newness of today's full-fledged bourgeois sector among African Americans. The vast majority of the newly fledged black bourgeoisie (a bourgeoisie that is without or rather has fewer of the "pathologies" identified by Frazier) come from blue-collar or upper-working-class and lower-middle-class African American families, with only a small section of today's black bourgeoisie having second-generation bourgeois origin (perhaps 10 to 20 percent). Thus, most of the new black bourgeoisie continue to have overlapping class and cultural ties deep in the everyday realities of black ethnicity. They experience a kind of sociocultural asymmetry, a pattern also found in the upward mobility trajectories of such white ethnic groups as Irish Americans, Italian Americans, and Jewish Americans.

Be this as it may, owing to both residual racism among white Americans and sociocultural asymmetry patterns among African Americans, the insider/outsider aspect of status-deracialization among the post-Frazier black bourgeoisie indicates that status-deracialization is quite problematic. It is not always easy to function as a member of the post-Frazier black bourgeoisie today, for it is a mercurial ethnic class. However, given African Americans' origins in slavery and their travail under a century of white supremacist patterns down to the 1960s, the current "split-personality" pressures facing some members of today's black bourgeoisie are a comparatively minor burden to bear, I suggest.

In addition to status-deracialization as a new systemic feature or dynamic associated with the post-Frazier black middle-class and professional sector, the post-Frazier black bourgeois stratum has spawned a wholly new kind of class stratification dynamic among African American society. Owing to the qualitatively new level of nationwide job markets, nationwide higher education institutional access, and access to competitive income and overall compensation, the post-Frazier black bourgeoisie has fashioned a systemically stronger position for itself within African American society. And this stronger position for the post-Frazier black bourgeoisie has, in turn, been curiously reinforced by the mobility ceiling that residual neoracist patterns in American society have imposed on the lower-stratum sector of African American households (the weak working-class and poor households) that make up nearly 40 percent of such households. Andrew Billingsley, an African American sociologist, has organized data that illustrate well the job-market and income basis of this new kind of class stratification dynamic among African American society. These data are shown in table 3.

A corollary set of data organized by Billingsley is shown in table 4. These data suggest a growing differential within the African American social system in terms of what might be called societal efficacy among class or status ranks. For example, of all black families, the 9 percent in the upper class include 96 percent husband/wife families; the 27 percent middle-class black families include 83 percent husband/wife families; and the 34 percent working-class non-poor families include 60 percent husband/wife families. But working-class

Table 3
Social-Class Structure of African-American Families, 1969–1986

	1969		1983		1986	
	Families	%	Families	%	Families	%
Upper Class	143,000	3	267,000	4	624,000	9
Middle Class	1,100,000	25	1,500,000	25	1,910,000	27
Working Class Nonpoor	2,100,000	44	2,400,000	36	2,420,000	34
Working Class Poor	688,000	14	963,000	14		
Under-Class Nonworking Poor	716,000	14	1,500,000	23	2,142,000	30

SOURCE: Andrew Billingsley, "Understanding African-American Family Diversity," in the STATE OF BLACK AMERICA 1990 (National Urban League, New York, 1990)

poor households are 67 percent single-parent families, and among underclass households, 75 percent are single-parent families.

Ultimately, the new politicization capability of the post-Frazier black bourgeoisie will enable it to influence both the public policy and private power sectors in American society to upgrade the status of the weak working-class and poor sector among African Americans. This politicization was one of the important transformations in the systemic character of the post-Frazier black elite.

Concluding Note: Politicization of Post-Frazier Black Bourgeoisie

As I've already suggested, the critical thrust of Frazier's keen analysis of upper-stratum African Americans (the middle-class and professional sector) focused on this stratum's "societal dimensions,"

Table 4
African-American Social Class and Family Structure

Class	*Family Structure*		
	Married Couple	Single-Parent	Working Wife
Upper Class	96%	04%	50%
Middle Class	83%	17%	78%
Working Class (Nonpoor)	60%	40%	45%
Working Class (Poor)	33%	67%	33%
Underclass (Nonworking Poor)	25%	75%	25%

SOURCE: Andrew Billingsley, "Understanding African-American Family Diversity," in the STATE OF BLACK AMERICA 1990 (National Urban League, New York, 1990)

the dimensions that exhibited the "pathologies" Frazier pinpointed for a very good reason. Namely, because during the first fifty years in the development of the black bourgeoisie, this leadership sector of African American society was prevented by American racist patterns from fashioning for itself a parallel "political dimension." Thus, while the systemic strengthening of the social structural attributes of the black bourgeoisie or upper stratum was a crucial aspect of developments during the post-Frazier era from late 1960s to the present, an equally important aspect of the post-Frazier era has been the full-fledged politicization of the black bourgeoisie. This development E. Franklin Frazier, writing in the early 1950s, could not have possibly foreseen. Indeed, Frazier wrote *Black Bourgeoisie* under the assumption that viable political incorporation of African American citizens in the American mainstream would not likely occur during the twentieth century.

It is important to recognize that an important structural difference between the African American middle-class and professional elements, on the one hand, and the bourgeoisie among white ethnic groups, on the other hand, during the long period between World War I and the 1970s, was that white ethnic groups had a three-generation lead time in reinforcing their sociostructural development with access to political power at both the local and national levels of American politics. While white groups in the era between

World War I and the 1960s were pursuing viable electoral empowerment and advancing to the next political development stage, which I call power consolidation politics, the African American community —some twelve million strong by 1930, twenty million by the 1950s— was largely confined to protest politics. During that period, the NAACP, the National Urban League, black professional associations, activist religious bodies, activist civic associations, and some activist black trade unions like A. Philip Randolph's Brotherhood of Sleeping Car Porters were the African American population's conveyer belts of protest politics, what after World War II was dubbed civil rights movement politics.

Black protest politics' task was to smash the rigidity and systemic viciousness of American racist patterns—epitomized from the 1890s to the 1950s by nearly four thousand recorded lynchings. Even so, ending systemic racism ultimately required massive federal judicial and legislative intervention (e.g., Civil Rights Acts of 1963 and 1964, the Voting Rights Act of 1965, etc.) before the African American bourgeoisie could fashion viable electoral empowerment politics, with a cutting-edge role played by newly elected black mayors from 1967/1968 onward, and move toward power consolidation politics. By the early 1960s, there were fewer than three hundred black elected officials in the United States (for a black population of about twenty million), six of whom were in Congress—five in the House of Representatives and one, Edward Brooke of Massachusetts, in the Senate. But seven years after the Voting Rights Act of 1965, there were about four thousand black elected officials and today there are over eight thousand—some 2 percent of all elected officials nationwide. When perhaps thirty thousand or so appointed and civil service officials are added, the aggregate African American political class today totals nearly forty thousand.

Thus, new electoral empowerment and new power consolidation politics developments, from the 1970s through the 1990s, produced a kind of generic liberalism tilt to the political orientation of the African American middle-class and professional sector. The electoral empowerment thrust that commenced in the late 1960s was linked to the liberal wing of the Democratic party during the Kennedy and Johnson administrations, and this black elite/liberal Democratic party linkage was reinforced during the Carter administration (1976 to 1980), and even more strongly reinforced during the two terms of the Clinton administration (1992 to 2000). Under the Clinton administration, the African American professional class hit its peak in national political power thus far: three cabinet positions during the first Clinton administration (Commerce, Labor, Transportation), as well as important second-level executive positions, which included assistant secretary of defense, assistant secretary of state for African affairs, Federal Communications Commission director, director of Office of Management of the Budget, director of the Department of Justice's Civil Rights Division.

These developments in the political power consolidation capability of the post-Frazier era have, I suggest, ensured, at least for the short run, a generic liberalism orientation within the majority wing of the black bourgeoisie. Today the bourgeoisie among none of the white ethnic groups in American society registers as strong and as consistent liberal political orientation, measured by the degree of support for liberal Democratic party policies, as does the post-Frazier black bourgeoisie.[5] And the strong democratic liberalism of the black bourgeoisie today has trickled down, as it were, through middle and lower strata African American households. Today, no serious expectations of presidential electoral victory by a Democratic party candidate is conceivable without the full backing of African American voters. I like to think that had he lived, E. Franklin Frazier would have been pleased.

5. For an evaluation of the politicization of the post-Frazier black bourgeoisie, see Martin Kilson, "State of African-American Politics," in *The State of Black America 1998*, ed. Lee A. Daniels (New York: National Urban League, 1998).

E. Franklin Frazier's Role in African Studies

MICHAEL R. WINSTON

E. Franklin Frazier was one of the world's leading social scientists.[1] Perhaps now best known as the author of *Black Bourgeoisie,* a controversial study of what he described as a new social class among American Negroes, his distinction as a scholar rests on other works. Of his ten books, *The Negro Family in the United States* (1939) has been justly regarded for many years as a research classic of the "golden age" of American sociology. The canon of social science investigation of race relations also includes his authoritative and comprehensive synthesis *The Negro in the United States* (1949). Perhaps less well known today are his empirical studies of race relations in Brazil and the Caribbean published in the 1940s.[2] Even more obscure, unfortunately, are Frazier's contributions to the then-embryonic multidisciplinary study of modern Africa.

This paper will treat briefly Frazier's approach to African studies, with special emphasis on his attempt to develop a coherent intellectual matrix for understanding the rapid social and economic

1. See Edwards, *Frazier on Race Relations,* vii–xx; G. Franklin Edwards, "E. Franklin Frazier: Race, Education and Community" in *Sociological Traditions from Generation to Generation,* ed. Robert K. Merton and Matilda White Riley (Norwood, N.J.: Ablex Publishing, 1980), 109–29; and G. Franklin Edwards, "Frazier, E[dward] Franklin (1894–1962)" in *The Dictionary of American Negro Biography,* ed. Rayford W. Logan and Michael R. Winston (New York: W. W. Norton, 1982), 241–44. The most detailed account of his career is in Platt, *Frazier Reconsidered.*

2. See, for example, Frazier, "Negro Family in Bahia, Brazil," 465–78; "Some Aspects of Race Relations in Brazil" *Phylon* 3 (1942): 284–95; "A Comparison of Negro-White Relations in Brazil and in the United States," *Transactions of the New York Academy of Sciences* (May 1944): 251–69; and "Race Relations in the Caribbean," in *The Economic Future of the Caribbean,* ed. E. Franklin Frazier and Eric Williams (Washington: Howard University Press, 1944): 27–31.

changes in sub-Saharan Africa in the 1950s. It will also attempt to demonstrate that one of his major claims in *Black Bourgeoisie,* that the American Negro intellectual was an abject "failure," developed at least in part from his encounter with African intellectuals during the late flowering of his interest in the social and political problems of African decolonization.

E. Franklin Frazier was one of a small group that founded the African Studies Association. His colleagues were William O. Brown, Alan Pifer, William Hance, Gwendolen Carter, Ruth Sloan, Jean Comhaire, George Carpenter, and L. Gray Cowan. The first formal meeting launching the ASA was held at the Roosevelt Hotel in New York in March 1957. Elected to the association's first board of directors, Frazier was vice president (and president-elect) at the time of his death in May 1962.

Although he was one of the most respected sociologists of his time, Frazier's role in founding the African Studies Association may be puzzling to those unfamiliar with the evolution of his scholarship or the African studies field. Prior to 1955 he had not published any articles, scholarly or popular, on Africa. He could not be described accurately as an "Africanist" in contemporary usage. Yet, on closer investigation, it is evident that he had a long interest in African history, culture, and society. Like others of his generation of black American intellectuals, Frazier experienced the remarkable revival of interest in Africa that was a significant aspect of the "Harlem Renaissance" of the 1920s. He was, in fact, a contributor (not on an African subject) to *The New Negro: An Interpretation,* edited by one of his former professors at Howard, Alain LeRoy Locke. In the context of this essay it is worth recalling that in his introduction Locke asserted that one characteristic of the New Negro was "the consciousness of acting as the advance-guard of the African peoples in their contact with Twentieth Century civilization."[3]

Although he rejected firmly and unequivocally the aesthetic romanticism about Africa that was associated with the Harlem Renaissance, as well as the "Back to Africa" black nationalism of Marcus Garvey, Frazier was an American Negro intellectual concerned primarily with the development of a realistic and objective understanding of modern Africa. The best documentary evidence respecting

3. Frazier, "Durham," in *The New Negro,* 233–40, 14.

Frazier's evolving interest in Africa is in his papers in the manuscript division of the Moorland-Spingarn Research Center at Howard University. In the section of his papers labeled "Academic Notes," for example, one finds a paper that he wrote for an anthropology course at the University of Chicago in 1927 entitled "The Family among Some Tribes in the East African Cattle Area."[4] The study earned the grade of "A," but like most graduate student papers, it understandably does not bear the closest scrutiny more than sixty years later. It is a highly detailed, solidly factual study, with—mirabile dictu—virtually no opinion or interpretation. Its real significance is its demonstration of Frazier's early academic interest in a field in which he would not venture publication until more than twenty-five years later.

From a methodological standpoint it is a particularly hazardous if not an entirely dubious exercise to attempt to trace the evolution of a scholar's interest in a subject. There are, of course, some hints in published work, but the source of the interest, and the factors involved in intensifying it over time, are especially elusive. It is probably sufficient to state that prior to the late 1940s or early 1950s, Frazier's professional interest in Africa focused mainly on the impact of the African slave trade on American society, especially its pathological consequences in plantation society in the southern United States. Related to the constellation of issues concerning the institution of slavery in the United States was the matter of "African survivals," which he debated vigorously with his friend Melville Herskovits in the 1940s.[5] The main point is that Frazier's publications before the 1950s were more concerned with Africa in terms of historical "background" for the study of black American social institutions, especially the family, than with Africa as a primary subject for research.

While I have no thesis to argue in this respect, I would suggest that in the case of his African interests Frazier's political concerns antedated his scholarly investigations. Although he frequently insisted that he was a "scientist" of society, no more, no less, E. Franklin Frazier was far from an "ivory tower" academic. He succeeded in keeping his academic and political interests separate most of the time,

4. Frazier Papers, box 131–1, folder 21.

5. See Melville J. Herskovits, *The Myth of the Negro Past* (New York: Harper & Bros., 1942); E. Franklin Frazier, "Significance of the African Background," in *Negro in the United States* (1957), 3–21.

but in the case of Africa he was clearly committed to decolonization and the development of independent African states long before he began to write professionally in this area. Frazier tended to characterize European imperialism in his more cautious scholarship as a phase of "the expansion of Europe," but a close reading of his work compels the conclusion that he saw clearly the connection between white supremacy in the southern United States and its kindred political and economic institutions in Asia, Africa, and the Caribbean.

E. Franklin Frazier was part of the militant intellectual opposition to European imperialism many years before it became United States policy to accept African decolonization. With many of his black contemporaries, he recognized European imperialism as the trunk of a system whose branches extended globally to include most forms of white subordination of nonwhite populations. Important evidence of this is Frazier's participation (in September 1921) in the Paris session of the Second Pan-African Congress organized by W. E. B. Du Bois.[6] Frazier was then in Europe as a fellow of the American Scandinavian Foundation to study the system of folk high schools in Denmark.

In 1941, Frazier joined the Council on African Affairs, an organization incorporated in that year (but founded in 1937) with the stated purpose of providing "accurate information on the conditions and struggles of the peoples of Africa and to promote and support their welfare and efforts toward liberation." Frazier had been invited to join the council only one month after its incorporation. In his letter inviting Frazier to become a member of the council, Max Yergan, executive director, wrote that there was "particular desire on the Council to have you join it not only because of your general interest in Africa but in order that the Council may have the benefit of your help in formulating and carrying out our program of research and publication." At the time that Frazier joined the council it had only fourteen members, including officers. Paul Robeson had become chairman in 1941.[7]

6. W. E. B. Du Bois, *Dusk of Dawn: An Essay toward an Autobiography of a Race Concept* (New York: Harcourt, Brace & World, 1940), 260–68, 274–78; and Rayford W. Logan, "The Historical Aspects of Pan-Africanism: A Personal Chronicle," *African Forum* (summer 1965): 90–104.

7. Frazier Papers, box 131–30, "Council on African Affairs." The center's manuscript division also holds the papers of Paul Robeson and Max Yergan,

The council's early emphasis on accurate information was intended to make it possible for "the American people [to] play their proper part in the struggle for African freedom." Beginning in 1943 the council published *New Africa* and the "Spotlight on Africa Newsletter," issued monthly. During the 1940s the council's membership included a veritable "who's who" of American Negro scholars and public affairs leaders, including Rayford W. Logan, Mordecai W. Johnson, Mary McLeod Bethune, Alain Locke, Mary Church Terrell, J. Finley Wilson, and Ralph J. Bunche. As the political orientation of the organization moved further left after World War II, many of the early members resigned. Frazier remained, despite FBI and IRS harassment of the organization.

The council was, in fact, one of the early and influential American lobbying organizations mobilizing American public opinion against European colonialism in Africa. At the council's Conference on Africa in April 1944, for example, the resolutions opposed forced labor in Africa, urged the implementation of fair wages and the end of discrimination in employment and of unfair trading practices. The correspondence related to the Council on African Affairs in the Frazier papers at Howard demonstrates clearly Frazier's sharp rejection of retreat in the face of United States government intimidation. For those crucial meetings that he could not attend because of other obligations, he gave his proxy to Paul Robeson. When the council was scheduled for hearings in November 1953 before the Subversive Activities Control Board, the council issued a press release stating that it "categorically denies the Attorney General's allegation that it is a "Communist-front" organization." By 1955 the council had dissolved itself because "continuing Government harassment" made "further effective work by the organization impossible."[8]

As has been mentioned earlier, Frazier began rather early to take a comparative perspective on race relations. His studies of Brazil and the Caribbean in the 1940s provided an almost natural transition to his inclusion of Africa in his research, teaching, and writing a decade later. Several circumstances converged after World War II. Frazier's

---

but as of February 2000, the relevant files on the Council of African Affairs have been closed to researchers by the donors of the Yergan papers. See also Martin Bauml Duberman, *Paul Robeson* (New York: Alfred A. Knopf, 1988), 297, 340, 374, 684.

8. Frazier Papers, box 131–30, "Council on African Affairs."

association with the Council on African Affairs brought to his attention a wide range of political, economic, and social data not otherwise readily available in the 1940s. In 1951 he was appointed chief of the Division of Applied Social Sciences of UNESCO at its headquarters in Paris. One of his responsibilities was to organize seminars at the research institutes supported by UNESCO in Africa. He traveled widely in Africa and developed UNESCO research projects on the social impact of industrialization in Africa.[9] In addition to this stimulating field experience, Frazier met in Paris the group of Senegalese and other African intellectuals associated with the Society of African Culture and its outstanding journal, *Presence Africaine,* edited by Alioune Diop.

In 1954, a year after his return to the United States from France, Frazier established, with Rayford W. Logan and others, Howard's African studies program, later supported by a grant from the Ford Foundation.[10] At this time, Frazier began to teach courses on Africa in the department of sociology, including one on social change in Africa. He also taught this course regularly at the School of Advanced International Studies of the Johns Hopkins University after Vernon McKay organized an African studies program there in 1957.

From the early 1950s until his death in 1962, Frazier's contributions to the relatively new field of African studies included a modest number of research articles on urbanization and social change in Africa, the impact of colonialism on African social forms and personality, and African education.[11] Perhaps, even more important than these studies was his more extended treatment of Africa as part of the most ambitious work of his later career, *Race and Culture Contacts in the Modern World* (1957). In undertaking an analysis of Frazier's contribution to the study of modern Africa, I shall consider his journal articles along with this book.

E. Franklin Frazier approached Africa from the distinct perspective of sociology but with a disciplinary eclecticism generally in

9. Frazier Papers, box 131–1, "Personal Papers," folder 1.

10. For the development of African Studies in the United States in this period see Adelaide Cromwell Hill, "African Studies Programs in the United States" in *Africa from the Point of View of American Negro Scholars,* ed. Alioune Diop (Paris: Presence Africaine, 1958), 361–78.

11. Frazier had no work published on Africa as the primary subject of research until he was sixty-one years old. Between 1955 and his death in 1962, six articles and two chapters in books were published.

advance of his contemporaries. As far as he was concerned, for example, the historical processes that produced the contemporary situation in Africa were within the scope of the sociologist, not merely because they provided a means of grasping the evolution or "natural history" of social phenomena, but because they were essential for the creation of an intellectual structure that could pass the test of both relevance and explanatory potency.

Frazier was particularly dismayed by what he saw as the creeping trivialization of social science research by the retreat to relatively "safe" subjects and the elevation of methodology to a new academic mystique. It was clear to him that it was better to tackle a "big" research problem that did not lend itself to neat research design than to select relatively minor issues that could be contained within purely quantitative or "uncontaminated" but statistically elegant methodologies.[12] Even more exasperating to him was what he regarded as the retreat of social scientists from the study of problems that had major economic or political significance, a derivative effect of the political conservatism that gripped the United States at the height of the Cold War. What is perhaps Frazier's most considered statement of his view concerning this matter was included in a lecture series at the University of London in 1953:

> it is necessary to consider the relevance of economic and political factors to sociological study and research. Some sociologists, especially the majority of American sociologists, have regarded economic and political factors as irrelevant to sociological inquiry. They have generally confined their studies to the investigation of social interaction or the measurement and analysis of attitudes, or they have utilized some vague concept [such] as mores and folkways which they regarded as sui generis sociological phenomena. According to our point of view, sociological analysis must include economic and political factors relevant to the analysis of a particular system of social relations which is being studied.[13]

Frazier regarded nationalism, for example, as an object of sociological inquiry because it involves, in addition to its economic and political aspects, the problem of social organization and a cultural dimension that embraces a "transvaluation of values."[14]

12. See also, Edwards, "Frazier: Race, Education and Community," 119–20.
13. Frazier, "Theoretical Structure of Sociology," 294.
14. Ibid., 302–3.

In fact, Frazier's framework for studying modern Africa was even more extensive than what may be suggested by his conception of nationalism as being within the scope of sociology. "The sociological analysis of race and cultural contacts," he wrote, "must include the study of the influence of the geographic environment and the technological development of peoples as well as the effect of economic and political institutions upon the relations of men of different races and cultures. Therefore, it is necessary to draw upon the findings of all the social sciences: human geography, anthropology, economics and political science."[15] In addition to this multidisciplinary matrix, Frazier had a quasi-political conception of the "colored peoples of the world" that derived primarily, I think, from the early work of W. E. B. Du Bois.[16] Although not a well-developed or analytically precise concept, it had the intellectual function of placing the issues facing Africans in the 1950s within a larger context of nonwhite peoples who had been either directly subjugated or otherwise exploited by Europeans and white Americans. This was a perspective not uncommon among many of Frazier's black contemporaries, but there was little evidence of it among the emerging professional Africanists of that era, most of whom were white. I see, therefore, a linkage between Frazier's analytic framework of "race and culture contacts" and his political construct of "the colored peoples of the world." This inference is based on Frazier's expanding intellectual interests in that period and his views about the Cold War, which are probably not now well known. The following analysis by Frazier will illustrate the point:

> The present crisis in the relation of the white and colored peoples of the world has developed as a phase of the profound change in the power relations of the peoples of the modern world. This change in the power relations of the modern world has been developing since World War I. It was, however, as the result of World War II that the centers of power in the modern world shifted from western Europe to the Soviet Union and the United States. During World War II, the United States became the dominant industrial and financial as well as

15. Frazier, *Race and Culture,* 31.

16. The concept was not limited, of course, to Du Bois. See, for example, G. Spiller, ed., *Papers on Inter-Racial Problems Communicated to the First Universal Races Congress Held at the University of London, July 26–29, 1911* (London: P. S. King & Son, 1911).

> military power in the world. At the same time, the Soviet Union was able not only to gain control of eastern Europe but to secure the support of Asians by aiding them in their revolt against European domination. These two powers, the United States and the Soviet Union, are struggling to win the support of the peoples of the world who are not under their control. The peoples who are not under the control of these two power systems are mainly the colored peoples of the world who have either recently secured their independence, including most of the peoples of southeast Asia, or who have begun their struggle for independence or a greater amount of self-determination, including the people of Africa.[17]

Frazier's conception of the Cold War's impact on the nonwhite colonies of the world was also reinforced by a significant development of the mid-1950s. At the time that he was writing *Race and Culture Contacts in the Modern World* there was a growing expectation that countries with a similar experience of European political and economic control could be transformed into a new geopolitical reality, namely an Afro-Asian power bloc. Frazier noted in this book, for example, that "the colored peoples of the world are developing a solidarity of interest which is based in part upon race consciousness. This was dramatized at the Asian-African Conference in Bandung, Indonesia. In his opening speech on April 18, 1955, President Soekarno stated almost at the beginning: 'As I survey this hall, and the distinguished guests gathered here, my heart is filled with emotion. This is the first intercontinental conference of coloured peoples in the history of mankind!' "[18]

Throughout his discussion of Africa in *Race and Culture Contacts in the Modern World,* Frazier oscillates between the poles of structural analysis and political commentary. Moreover, a substantial part of his discussion of Africa in that book has little to do specifically with race or culture *contacts* as such. West African states such as Ghana (then the Gold Coast) and Nigeria receive more attention than do South Africa or Kenya, where "racial frontiers" were far more significant and directly relevant to Frazier's central theses about race and culture contacts.

There can be little doubt that Frazier brought to his work on Africa an especially broad scope of inquiry. Additionally, he approached

17. Frazier, *Race and Culture,* 226.
18. Ibid., 337

the enormous quantities of data within that scope from a structural point of view. An example of this is his discussion of the economic aspects of European domination in various geographic settings, such as the coastal trading areas of West Africa, the East African agricultural highlands, and the mines in South Africa. To create a coherent framework for comparison of situations that differed mainly in details rather than essentials, Frazier introduced interpretive "structures." An illustration of this is his use of the concept of "the ecological basis of race relations."

> The ecological basis of race relations is concerned with the manner in which the relations of men to their environment determine relationship patterns which develop between men with different racial and cultural backgrounds. Although the adjustments of men to their environment is always achieved in terms of cultural heritage, it happens that when men with different racial and cultural backgrounds confront each other, the accommodation which is established between them is on a physical and biological plane.[19]

Arguing that the ecological organization formed a kind of "symbiotic substructure" on which economic, political, and cultural activities rested, Frazier attempted to examine functionally the evolution of racially hegemonic systems. From the uncoordinated and improvised "Wild West" beginnings of racial conquest in the western United States or South Africa to its more systematic and sophisticated forms of economic and political exploitation in modernizing cities and nations, Frazier saw a structural continuum that was determinative of the social relations between groups. Frazier used a wide range of examples to demonstrate this, from the Dutch colonization of Indonesia to the British Raj in India, but it will no doubt be more appropriate here to observe the schematic application of his model to the South African case:

> South Africa is a country in the temperate zone in which Boer, English, Hottentot, Bushmen, Bantu, and Indians have struggled to survive. During this struggle the Bushmen were hunted as wild beasts and driven into the desert while the Hottentots became a dying race. The advance of Boers in search of water and grass brought them into conflict with the Bantu who sought the same sources of existence. Then

19. Ibid., 97

> in the closing years of the eighteenth century came the English with their ideas of freedom. Each advance of the European frontier failed to drive the Bantu away; each advance ended in making him a settler on European farms. The Great Trek of the Boers beyond British control only established new racial frontiers and made impossible the separation of white and black. The introduction of Indian laborers on the sugar plantations of Natal added to the complexity of the racial pattern of South Africa. The pattern of racial settlement was finally determined by industrialization and urbanization. The diamond fields changed the competition of whites and blacks for land and cattle into competition for a place in industry. Then came the gold rush on the Rand which made Johannesburg the largest city in Africa. Before 1923 the native population was ignored; but in that year an act was passed to segregate Europeans and natives. Despite subsequent acts the natives continued to enter Johannesburg and other cities. By 1946 nearly 1,800,000 natives were in the cities of the Union of South Africa.[20]

While this is a fair example of Frazier's schematized use of history and his "racial frontiers" thesis, it does not reflect his more complex approach to social change in modern Africa. To assess that one must turn to his more specialized studies of Africa in which he was not tied to the comparative schema that give structure and coherence (at an analytical price) to *Race and Culture Contacts in the Modern World*.

It is important to keep in mind that E. Franklin Frazier came to the field of African studies at a crucial but confusing period of political and social change, on the cusp of the emergence of independent African nations. Significantly, Frazier identified a cluster of research issues that remain important thirty years later, despite dramatic changes in the political and economic institutions of African societies. He was, first of all, interested in the impact of colonialism on African collective structures, which he called "social forms," and on the individual "African personality." He wanted to define systematically the sociological problems in African societies created by "the various types of economic exploitation and systems of social control through which African peoples have experienced the impact of Western civilization."[21]

20. Ibid., 96–97

21. E. Franklin Frazier, "The Impact of Colonialism on African Social Forms and Personality," in *Africa in the Modern World*, ed. Calvin Stillman (Chicago: University of Chicago Press, 1955), 70.

Frazier focused particularly on the massive dislocation of populations caused by the creation of large-scale plantation agriculture, notably cultivation of cacao in the Gold Coast and of groundnuts in Senegal. Mining operations were even more disruptive, he pointed out, as were the huge timber operations in the Belgian Congo, Kenya, and Nigeria. He cited the impact of labor mobilization systems employed by Europeans on age and sex distribution in rural areas and the concomitant disintegration of the traditional African family. Frazier also noted the transformation of traditional values as the collectivism of most African traditional societies was steadily undermined by the individualism fostered by industrialization and urbanization. Traditional African values and social forms were under siege from two intersecting sources, modernization as such and the reality of white domination. The racial aspect of this combination, he maintained, had "an undoubtedly traumatic effect upon the personality of the African." "To the African," he continued, "European civilization is not alone a different social organization and a different system of values; it is the proof of the superiority of white men over black men. No teaching of racial pride or encouragement of native arts on the part of the white man can remove the implication of black inferiority." Frazier did not, however, posit simply a pathological model of African personality caught between conflicting forces of traditional values and modernization under colonial auspices. Regarding the western educated African as inevitably a type of "marginal man," Frazier argued that the educated African had the option to "escape from the traumatic effects of white domination" by becoming the leader of a nationalistic movement or by adopting a "revolutionary ideology." In this way he placed nationalistic and revolutionary movements in a frame of reference that was within the traditional disciplinary boundaries of sociology while simultaneously making a *sub silentio* political statement.[22]

In his research on Africa, Frazier also continued some of the thematic interests he had developed much earlier, particularly the impact of urbanization on rural folk. As he conceived of urbanization, it was inevitably a solvent of traditional folk values and associations. It is not surprising to observe his application of this model to Africa. The African city was for him the place where Africans

22. Ibid., 95.

would achieve a new level of consciousness, first on social issues, then on the larger ones of national integration and participation in the competitive world of nation-states. "As their tribal exclusiveness is broken down and ethnic identifications are lost," he wrote, "Africans are developing a wider social consciousness and a new identification. Nothing offers a better means to attain this larger social consciousness and new identification than nationalism." As Frazier analyzed the process of social change in the Africa of the 1950s, the social forces propelled by industrialization and urbanization could be shaped by public policy to enhance nation building, a kind of compensatory balance to the destructive impact of these forces on traditional values and institutions.[23]

E. Franklin Frazier did not live to witness the rapid change in Africa's political leadership that occurred in the 1960s. He was particularly, and uncharacteristically, optimistic about the future of African leadership because of his association with Nkrumah in Ghana and Azikiwe in Nigeria. He was also impressed with the African intellectuals he encountered in the 1950s who were grappling with the problems of culture, modernization, and the future relations of Africa to the Western world. In his last published article, "The Failure of the Negro Intellectual," he sharply contrasts what he regarded as the alienation of the American Negro intellectual from "the masses" and the new African intellectual. According to Frazier, black American intellectuals had been coopted by a superficial view of the world espoused by the new "black bourgeoisie" while African intellectuals were engaged in tasks of enduring significance. Black American intellectuals had, he wrote, "failed to dig down into the experiences of the Negro and provide the soul of a people" while the "African intellectual recognizes what colonialism has done to the African and he sets as his first task the mental, moral, and spiritual rehabilitation of the African."[24]

Frazier's view of the relation of black Americans to Africa was not, of course, confined to intellectuals. One of the important developments of the 1950s was an increasing relationship of significant

23. E. Franklin Frazier, "Urbanization and Social Change in Africa," *SAIS Review* (winter 1959): 8; E. Franklin Frazier, "Urbanization and Its Effects upon the Task of Nation Building in Africa," *Journal of Negro Education* (July 1961): 214–22.

24. Frazier, "Failure of the Negro Intellectual," 34–35.

numbers of black Americans with Africa and organizations, private and government, whose purpose was the enhancement of the "new Africa" that was to emerge from the legacy left by European colonialism. Frazier was dubious about this entire development. He thought that much of this rested "upon sentimental grounds" or represented "a type of wishful thinking."[25] Recapitulating in the main the argument that he had developed in his book *Black Bourgeoisie,* Frazier dismissed out of hand the potential contributions American Negroes could make to African development. Further, he alleged that Negro artists and intellectuals were "sterilized" by an inability to come to terms with the culture of the Negro folk, which represented the real "soul" of the race, as well as the dilemmas posed by being a disadvantaged minority in a white society. Citing what he characterized as a lack of "intellectual or spiritual freedom" caused by the "entire separate institutional life" of American segregation, Frazier argued that American Negroes could not assist in the development of Africa. He also pursued the theme that the marginality of blacks in American society contributed also to a misunderstanding of what was at stake in the Cold War:

> as a result of his psychological and social isolation and his acceptance of the smugness and cheap values of the middle classes, American Negro intellectuals and artists seem to be ignorant or unconscious of the cultural problems which concern artists and intellectuals in the modern world. They have become mere parrots or phonograph records repeating the ideas of reactionary and conservative white people. There are rare exceptions, like W. E. B. Du Bois and Paul Robeson, but they are considered dangerous by white people, therefore, middle class Negroes regard them as dangerous.[26]

Convinced that "the African has a future in the world and has a place in shaping a new world as an African," Frazier also believed that American Negroes were prepared to reject their African origin and their cultural identity as the price for "acceptance by white Americans."[27] I have interpreted this remarkably pessimistic article as a reflection of Frazier's personal despair in the late 1950s about

25. Frazier, "What Can the American Negro Contribute?" in *Africa from the Point of View of American Negro Scholars,* 264.
26. Ibid., 276
27. Ibid., 278

the stalemate in race relations and the political and cultural conservatism that dominated American society. If that interpretation is correct, Frazier was seriously misled by the bitterness of his own isolation, both as a scholar and as an American citizen harassed by U.S. government agencies because of his political views. Frazier's characterization of American Negro intellectuals, for example, could not apply to the distinguished group of contributors to the volume in which this essay appeared. One could easily argue the reverse of Frazier's thesis and state that few white Americans could match the political sophistication and intellectual cosmopolitanism of that group.[28] It is also interesting to contrast Frazier's view of the American Negro's relation to Africa with some African views, especially the group of intellectuals that Frazier admired. Two years before Frazier's essay on this subject was published, Mrs. Alioune Diop of *Presence Africaine* wrote to Frazier to enlist his support in encouraging American Negro intellectuals to participate in the Congress of Black Writers and Artists to be held in Paris from September 19 to 22, 1956. She wrote that it would be "heartbreaking" (*navrant*) if American Negro intellectuals did not participate, since "no one can ignore the exceptional importance of the American Negro experience in the liberation of the mind of black people."[29]

E. Franklin Frazier did not claim to be a prophet, so he should not be taxed with failing to anticipate the remarkable efflorescence of black American interest in Africa that occurred in the years after his death in 1962. Yet it remains true that he greatly underestimated the changes that were in progress in the late 1950s with respect to the linkages between American Negroes and Africa. The evidence suggests that as Frazier became more disappointed with the racial situation in the United States and what he saw as the triumph of meretricious values among middle-class Negroes, he increasingly invested Africa with compensatory optimism. He hoped that in Africa black intellectuals would develop "a new conception of human relations and of the relations of men to the resources of the

28. Contributors to the volume included St. Clair Drake, Hugh H. Smythe, Lorenzo Dow Turner, James A. Porter, Samuel Allen, Mercer Cook, Rayford W. Logan, Horace Mann Bond, W. E. B. Du Bois, John W. Davis, Adelaide Cromwell Hill, Dorothy B. Porter, and Ulyssess Lee.

29. Mrs. Alioune Diop to Frazier, May 25, 1956, Frazier Papers, box 131–43, folder 2.

world, and thus enable mankind to achieve a new stage in the evolution of humanity."[30] In his hopes for the future of Africa, and a new world order in which imperialism and racism had been destroyed, E. Franklin Frazier demonstrated that although he was ever the intellectually daring loner, he was also a citizen of a world that has not yet come into being.

30. E. Franklin Frazier, "Message to the Congres' Des Ecrivains et Artistes Noirs" Sept. 4, 1956, Frazier Papers, box 131–43, folder 2.

Conclusion and Some Research Questions

JAMES E. TEELE

In this section, effort is made first to briefly comment on the contributions of our authors and second to offer suggestions for further research stimulated by the contributors. We begin with the recollections. John Hope Franklin, who served as chairman of the advisory board of President William Clinton's "Initiative on Race" (1997–2000), was one of Frazier's students at Fisk University in the early 1930s. John Hope Franklin's experience with Frazier clearly demonstrated the responsibility not only for scholarship but for commitment and leadership that Frazier demanded of his young undergraduates. Hylan Lewis, a member of Howard University's sociology department when Frazier took over as chairman in 1935, also shed much light on Frazier's experiences, and his problems, in his early years there. Lewis, privy to many of Frazier's tactics and frustrations as chairman at Howard, shared them with us in his essay, one of the last he wrote. Adelaide Cromwell, who knew Frazier when he taught at Howard, provided insights gleaned from her many conversations with him.

The memories related by Franklin, Lewis, and Cromwell allow us insight into some of the slights, the stresses, and the disappointments, as well as the triumphs that were the building blocks of Frazier's life. They also reflect the warmth and generosity that were essential parts of Frazier's character.

In part two, Robert Hall described Frazier's graduate experience at the University of Chicago under Robert Park, Ernest W. Burgess, and the other members of the sociology department and focused especially on Park's influence on Frazier with his theory of race relations. Hall noted some of the tensions in the department at the University of Chicago as seen by students of Ogburn, Stouffer, Thomas,

Park, and Burgess, and suggested that Frazier's views on change later veered away from Park's evolutionary views, becoming more radical.[1]

In part three, our authors took a close look at Frazier's analysis of the black bourgeoisie. Anthony Platt and John Bracey paid particular attention to Frazier's intentions as well as to his book's contributions to knowledge.

Platt noted that Frazier's concern with the black middle class was not a suddenly emerging phenomenon and that Frazier had been thinking and writing about the black middle class and black professionals for about forty years! Platt skillfully showed how Frazier's continued interest in change led to new awareness and new efforts to develop strategies and programs. These include, of course, very early efforts to understand and to galvanize the Negro middle class. It seems that there is no mystery and that no "motivation" has to be sought to explain why Frazier wrote *Black Bourgeoisie.* The book was a natural outcome of his efforts and his frustrations with the lack of change that he perceived in the situation of the black masses and in the behavior of their leaders.

Platt also observed that Frazier's disappointment with the black bourgeoisie included black religious leaders and noted that when Frazier was writing his last book, which was on the black church, he failed to see the prominent role played by the black church in the civil rights movement in the mid-1950s. Frazier had seen the agency potential of the Garvey movement, so it is surprising that his search for agency did not focus more on the African American church as an agency-laden institution. (In an insightful paper, Aldon Morris has hinted that only recently have scholars focused on the connection between social movements and the historic African American church leadership in the struggle for justice.)[2]

Frazier's willingness to take unpopular positions—defending Robeson, standing by Du Bois when others deserted him, exposing students to Marxist philosophy during the height of McCarthyism, and writing *Black Bourgeoisie*—was enthusiastically taken up

1. Stanford Lyman made a similar point about Frazier's views on change theory. See Stanford Lyman, *The Black American in Sociological Thought: A Failure of Perspective,* 62–67.

2. Aldon Morris, "Reflections on Social Movement Theory: Criticisms and Proposals," *Contemporary Sociology* 29, 3 (2000): 445–54.

by John Bracey in his analysis of Frazier's controversial book. One sees Frazier's commitment to the black community reflected in his dedication to teaching black students in black colleges. Once more, it is clear that there is no mystery, no need to search in corners for Frazier's motivation in writing *Black Bourgeoisie.*

It is interesting to note here that Bracey suggested Karl Marx's class analysis was stretched beyond recognition by Frazier's opinion that the black bourgeoisie had failed to exert leadership in the black community. (Here, Frazier could have responded that many leaders of past revolutions had, in fact, been from the upper class and that he was simply pointing out this model for change!) Bracey traced Frazier's long line of disappointments and found within it evidence that Frazier was constantly searching for programs for the liberation of black people in America.

While most of our authors dwelled on Frazier's strengths, Martin Kilson and Wornie Reed lost little time in pointing out the shortcomings in his work. Reed suggested that Frazier might have expected much too much from his "new black middle class," comprising as it did so few members. While Frazier suggested that the black middle class had grown, Reed showed that the size of the black male middle class, when compared with the white middle class, had not grown at all, had, indeed, shrunk in proportionate size, and suggested that Frazier's preoccupation with the black middle class led him to overlook the increasing unemployment rate of black males.

Kilson's highly trenchant critique found a couple of severe shortcomings in Frazier's *Black Bourgeoisie.* Kilson found that Frazier's conceptual framework was too heavily tilted to the "social-operation" dimension of the bourgeoisie and seemed to gloss over the important "power" dimension. He argued that the lack of access to capitalist structures retarded the modernization of a functional Afro-American community subsystem and that Frazier's narrow focus led him not only to suggest that the black community was pathological, but also to blame black leadership as irresponsible, playful, and living in a world of make-believe. He considered that Frazier exaggerated the extent to which the bourgeoisie engaged in consumerism and did not give credit to many of the progressive, positive efforts of the old black bourgeoisie. Indeed, Kilson excoriated Frazier for his underestimation of the contributions of black women, especially in the business world. Kilson then set out to correct some of Frazier's exaggerations and to show some of the constructive efforts of many of the black bourgeoisie. So while Reed differed with Frazier in regard to cause of the community's problems ("contemporary" discrimination rather than "historical" slavery), Kilson suggested that Frazier's portrait is off base, that capitalist power should have engaged more of Frazier's attention, and that Frazier should have opened his eyes to the hugely constructive role played by black women. (In a recent critique, Cheryl Gilkes mirrors some of Kilson's objections to Frazier's treatment of the roles and contributions of black women to the family and the community. Gilkes points out that Frazier has pulled a surprising switch by altering his earlier views in which he clearly recognized the strengths of black women.)[3]

Perhaps Frazier would reply to his critics that while he had certainly recognized the egalitarian nature of middle-class black homes in the past, this was not a solution to the abject lack of leadership shown by contemporary black males. He might argue that too many black women were content to "party" and to "dress up" during a period when the black masses were suffering and that by doing so they were aiding the laissez-faire behavior of their husbands, who were making believe that all was right in the black community in the early 1950s.

Frankly, Frazier was neither the first writer nor the last to be concerned about the problems of the black masses. Du Bois, to name one, preceded him and no doubt was his role model. Although Du Bois seemed to retreat from his earlier emphasis, it was he who emphasized in *The Souls of Black Folk* that the black intellectuals should take up leadership positions and guide the direction of the descendents of the freed slaves. However, Frazier, more than Du Bois, documented the devastating impact of slavery on blacks and the continuing problems faced by the black masses. Indeed, Frazier clearly demonstrated in his published works that American blacks had been engaged in a "long march" that stretched over centuries.

As Andrew Billingsley and others reminded us, Frazier was interested in far more than learning from the misadventures or failings

3. Cheryl Townsend Gilkes, "They Have Careers: Women, Class, and Families in the Sociology of E. Franklin Frazier" (Paper delivered at the Spotlight Panel cosponsored by the American Sociological Association and the Association of Black Sociologists, Washington, D.C., Aug. 14, 2000).

of black families; he was also interested in our learning from and applying the experiences of black families who succeeded in overcoming the continuing handicaps of slavery and its aftermath.[4] Frazier thought it imperative that the black middle class and intellectuals take the lead in this struggle.

The final chapter, by Michael Winston, is a reminder that Frazier was interested not just in the African American community, but also in black communities in far-off places: among them, Brazil and Africa. Indeed, after *Black Bourgeoisie* Frazier wrote *Race and Culture Contacts,* a work that demonstrates that he, like Du Bois, had a worldview and recognized that the strength of the future African American community might be in its knowledge of and ties to the larger black world. Winston noted that, debates with Herskovits aside, Frazier understood that if ties to Africa had been severed, there was good reason to renew them. So, far from a simple denigration of middle-class blacks, Winston suggested that Frazier's purpose might have been to shake them up and get this class to become what several of our authors noted has begun to transpire—a force for social change.

Recommendations for Further Research

Several issues or questions requiring research have been suggested by our contributors. In addition, some important tasks have been outlined by other scholars who have analyzed Frazier's work:

First, it has been claimed, for example, that Frazier largely ignored the constructive role played by black women in his criticism of them in *Black Bourgeoisie.* Was this a change from his earlier position, voiced in his earlier books? If so, what might have caused the change? Research in the Frazier archives at Howard's Moorland-Spingarn Center might shed light on this issue.

Second, what views do black scholars hold about the relations between African Americans and Africa today? What would be the next step in furtherance of a relationship? What model exists that would help to suggest a direction?

4. Andrew Billingsley, *Climbing Jacob's Ladder: The Enduring Legacy of African American Families* (New York: Simon & Schuster, 1992), 23. See also Hill, *African-American Family.*

A major research question concerns the extent to which conflict defines current black class relations. Walter Wallace has noted that several writers besides Frazier seemed to question whether American Negroes had a culture and whether if such culture existed, it was "healthy" or "pathological." Also, Wallace noted that an ancillary question (among many) was whether the black community possessed autonomous development.[5] Related to these issues is a question posed by August Meier in his review of *Black Bourgeoisie,* discussed earlier. Meier suggested that it is important to study further Frazier's "underlying hypothesis" that in their behavior the Negro masses and the Negro bourgeoisie each represent a distinct subculture in American society."[6] Kilson and others have argued strongly that there has been a growing interface between these two groups in the period since Frazier wrote his book. Thus, an important piece of research should focus on whether the black community is becoming more united in its outlook. In answering this question, special attention could be given to the roles played by gender and age.

In connection with this, it would be useful, for example, to ascertain the extent of black social class agreement concerning reparations and the manner of such payments. The question of reparations has received increased attention recently.[7]

Certainly, the contributors to this volume have each pointed to other unanswered questions concerning *Black Bourgeoisie* growing out of their own curiosity and interest in the book. It is hoped that their views and questions will encourage other scholars to examine the rich heritage of E. Franklin Frazier and perhaps to understand and extend the aspirations behind his work.

5. Walter Wallace, "Some Elements of Sociological Theory in Studies of Black Americans," in *Black Sociologists: Historical and Contemporary Perspectives,* ed. James Blackwell and Morris Janowitz, 299–321.

6. August Meier, "Some Observations on the Negro Middle Class," *Crisis* 64, 8 (Oct. 1958): 461–69, 517.

7. For example, see Randall Robinson, *The Debt: What America Owes to Blacks* (New York: Dutton, 2000); Joe R. Feagin, *Racist America: Roots, Current Realities, and Future Reparations* (New York: Routledge, 2000).

About the Contributors

John Hope Franklin is James B. Duke Professor of History Emeritus and for seven years was professor of legal history at Duke University's Law School. He graduated from Fisk University and received a Ph.D. in history from Harvard. Franklin has taught at several institutions, including Fisk, North Carolina Central, and Howard Universities. He joined the University of Chicago faculty in 1964 and was named John Matthews Manly Distinguished Service Professor in 1969. He has served as president of the Association of the Study of Afro-American Life and History, the Organization of American Historians, and Phi Beta Kappa.

His many works include *From Slavery to Freedom: A History of the African-Americans* and *The Color Line: Legacy for the Twenty-first Century.* In addition, he served as historical consultant on Steven Spielberg's Oscar-nominated film *Amistad.*

He served as chairman of the advisory board to President Clinton's Initiative on Race from 1997 to 1999, and he has received numerous awards, including the Jefferson Medal, the Presidential Medal, and the NAACP Spingarn Medal. In 1998 he was inducted into the North Carolina Literary Hall of Fame, and in 1999 Franklin became the first African American recipient of the Truman Good Neighbor Award.

Hylan A. Lewis received his undergraduate degree from Virginia Union University and his Ph.D. in sociology from the University of Chicago. Lewis was on the faculty at Howard University when E. Franklin Frazier became chairman in 1935. Later, he directed a child-rearing study for the Health and Welfare Council of the District of Columbia; the data from that study was used in *Tally's Corner* (by Elliot Liebow). In 1967, Lewis was appointed professor of sociology at Brooklyn College and a research associate at the Metropolitan Applied Research Center in New York. He was a visiting scholar at the Russell Sage Foundation and the author of *Blackways of Kent* and *Culture, Class and Poverty.* Lewis died while traveling in France in 2000.

Adelaide M. Cromwell received a B.A. from Smith College, an M.A. from the University of Pennsylvania, and a Ph.D. in sociology from Harvard. She served on the faculty of the African Research Center and in the department of sociology at Boston University before becoming the founding director of African American studies at Boston University; she directed that program until 1990 while still serving as a professor of sociology. She is now professor of sociology emeritus at Boston University. Her numerous publications include *The Other Brahmins: Boston's Black Upper Class 1750–1950* and *An African Victorian Feminist: The Life and Times of Adelaide Smith Casely Hayford, 1868–1960.*

Robert L. Hall received a B.A. from Harvard and a Ph.D. in history from Florida State University. He is currently director of African American studies at Northeastern University. Previously Hall
taught at Florida State University, the University of Maryland Baltimore County, and (as a visiting professor) at Rice University and George Mason University. He has been a fellow of the American Council of Learned Societies.

Hall's publications include *Do, Lord, Remember Me: Religion and the Forging of African-American Culture in Florida, 1565–1940.* He is currently working on a cultural history of the trans-Atlantic slave trade.

Anthony M. Platt is professor of social work at California State University, Sacramento, where he has taught since 1977. Previously, he taught at the University of California, Berkeley, and the University of Chicago. He received a B.A. from Oxford University and a Ph.D. in criminology from the University of California, Berkeley. He has been a visiting research associate at the Smithsonian's National Museum of American History and a visiting professor at the Institution of Comparative Law, Chuo University, Tokyo.

Among Platt's publications are *The Child Savers: The Invention of Delinquency* and *E. Franklin Frazier Reconsidered.* He is currently researching California's historiography.

John H. Bracey has been a member of the W. E. B. Du Bois Department of Afro-American Studies at the University of Massachusetts at Amherst since 1972. He previously taught Afro-American history at Northern Illinois University and the University of Rochester. He received a B.A. from Roosevelt University in Chicago and has done graduate work at Roosevelt and at Northwestern University. Bracey coedited (with August Meier and the late Elliott Rudwick) a number of volumes on various aspects of the Afro-American experience, including eight volumes in the series Explorations in the Black Experience, and (with Maurianne Adams) the anthology *Strangers and Neighbors: Relations between Blacks and Jews in the United States.* He is currently completing, with Ernest Allen, a six-volume documentary history titled *Unite or Perish: Black Nationalist and Radical Thought 1954–1974.* Bracey has also served as a consultant on video productions, among them treatments of W. E. B. Du Bois, Frederick Douglass, and A. Philip Randolph.

Wornie Reed received a Ph.D. in sociology from Boston University and is currently the director of the Urban Child Research Center at Cleveland State University. He has also served as director of the William Monroe Trotter Institute at the University of Massachusetts, Boston.

Reed edited a four-book series bearing on the status of African Americans, which includes the volumes *Research on African-American Families* and *Education of African-Americans.* He is president of the Association of Black Sociologists. He received an Emmy in 2000 for research in the development of a news series on cancer prevention.

Martin Kilson received his undergraduate training at Lincoln University in Pennsylvania and his Master's and Ph.D. from Harvard. He has taught at Harvard since 1962 and is Frank G. Thomson Research Professor there. Among Kilson's publications are *Apropos of Africa: Sentiments of American Negroes toward Africa 1850s to 1950s* (coedited with Adelaide Cromwell), *Political Change in a West African State,* and *The Making of Black Intellectuals: Studies on the African-American Intelligentsia* (forthcoming).

Michael R. Winston, a historian, is president of the Alfred Harcourt Foundation. Winston graduated magna cum laude from

Howard University, receiving his B.A., and was elected to Phi Beta Kappa. Subsequently, he was awarded the Moten Fellowship to study at the University of Edinburg and a Ford Foundation Faculty Fellowship, which allowed him to study at the Haus, Hof und Staatsarchiv in Vienna. Winston received a Ph.D. degree in European History from the University of California, Berkeley.

He was appointed to the Howard University faculty in 1964. From 1973 to 1983 he was director of the Moorland-Spingarn Research Center. He was appointed vice president for academic affairs in 1983, and he retired from Howard in 1990. In 1992 he became vice president of the Alfred Harcourt Foundation and in 1993, president.

From 1992 to 1993 he was chairman of the World History Committee of the National Council for History Standards and is currently a member of the Council on Foreign Relations.

Winston is coauthor, with Rayford W. Logan, of *The Negro in the United States,* volume 2, and coeditor, with Genna Rae McNeil, of *Historical Judgements Reconsidered.*

James E. Teele is professor of sociology at Boston University. He graduated from Virginia Union University, where he was a member of the first Foreign Study Team (Europe and Africa). He received a Ph.D. in sociology from New York University. Prior to joining the faculty of Boston University, he taught at New York University, the University of Aberdeen (Scotland), and Harvard. Teele has been a Russell Sage Foundation postdoctoral fellow, staff sociologist at the Judge Baker Guidance Center, and a scientist on the Medical Research Council of the United Kingdom. He was an organizer and forum member of the 1970 White House Conference on Children and served on review committees of the National Institute of Mental Health and the National Institute of General Medical Science. He was a member of the board of the American Hospital Association and of the Rockefeller Foundation's Advisory Committee for Single Parents.

He was an advisory editor of the *Encyclopedia of Sociology,* revised in 2000. Among his publications are *Mastering Stress in Child Rearing, The Evaluation of Operation Exodus: A School Bussing Program, Research on African-American Families,* and *Juvenile Delinquency* (editor).

Index

About the Editor

James E. Teele is Professor of Sociology and African American Studies at Boston University. He is the author, coauthor, or editor of six books, including *Evaluating School Busing: A Case Study of Boston's Operation Exodus*.